Blessings
Father Ken

The View from the Rectory Window
Volume II

Father Kenneth S. VanHaverbeke

D1275154

Artwork is from: http://clipart.christiansunite.com/

and from the Public Domain found at https://www.wpclipart.com/

ISBN: 151926254X
ISBN-13: 9781519262547

DEDICATION

To Father Pete Kovarik and Father Jerry Mullally,
my brother priests who taught me to live fully, love completely, and be the person God created me.
And to my father, John VanHaverbeke, who taught me to be a father.

CONTENTS

ACKNOWLEDGMENTS

In appreciation: to the Catholic Advance, Chris Riggs editor, who have graciously published these articles; to Denise Northup for proofreading; and to the many parishioners of the Diocese of Wichita who influenced my view from the rectory window.

All names have been changed in the following stories. Often circumstances, locations, and gender has also been changed in order to respect the privacy of those being written about.

INTRODUCTION

In the Year of the Priest 2009, I approached our editor of our diocesan newspaper, _The Catholic Advance_, to print a series of articles I named "_The View from the Rectory Window._" My goal was to share the ordinary life of a priest doing extra-ordinary things. The response was overwhelming and humbling.

Intending only to write articles for one year, the reaction of the readers encouraged me to continue to write about the joys and sorrows of the diocesan priesthood as I live it in the Diocese of Wichita (Kansas). I wish to thank the many individuals who took the time to e-mail, call, or write, giving me inspiration to continue writing.

In 2014 the first volume of these articles were published, and now a second volume is ready. In collecting these stories it is my hope to encourage young men to consider a life in the diocesan priesthood, and secondly to assist the faithful to appreciate how the life of the parish priest is often similar to that of a parent, with the joys and sorrows of a parent.

One of the wonders I've experienced in writing these reflections is how readers are surprised with the ordinariness of a priest's life. How even priests find it difficult to pray, just like parishioners. How we struggle with our boss (the bishop or pope) similar to anyone else might struggle with their boss. How we are irritated and sometimes bored with life. How human we priests are! I thought everyone knew!

Another wonder is how I continue to find stories how our Lord speaks to me through my life and ministry. All of us have stories of God working in our lives. It is really important for us to share these stories of God's love somehow to our families and friends. Often though, I find it easier to share stories of complaints about assignments, bishops, or brother priests rather than to express to my family, friends and parishioners how much I love the Lord and how I have experienced His love for me.

I am thankful for the parishioners who have encouraged me to share my priesthood through writing. Writing is prayer for me. Each night I pray for those whom the Lord has allowed me to serve these past 25 years of priesthood. I pray for those who have been touched by His Divinity through my ministry, but especially for those who have been hindered by my humanity.

May God continue to bless us, and may your future be filled with many opportunities of gratitude!

Father Ken VanHaverbeke
Easter 2016

1 THAT WHICH IS HIDDEN

"You are the light of the world. A city set on a mountain cannot be hidden. Nor do they light a lamp and then put it under a bushel basket; it is set on a lampstand, where it gives light to all in the house. Just so, your light must shine before others, that they may see your good deeds and glorify your heavenly Father." Matthew 5:14-16

The life of a priest sometimes parallels other professions. For instance a priest is called a Doctor of Souls. Or he might be a shepherd leading his flock. Or of a judge calling upon the wisdom of the ages to render a decision.

There are, however, other roles a parish priest assumes. A parking lot attendant trying to get all the cars parked for the Christmas Eve Mass. Or of a janitor when the toilet overflows. Or of a referee between two warring spouses. We are no different than any other father of a family. In fact, since our spouse is the church, we are a father of a family.

"For there is nothing hidden that will not be disclosed, and nothing concealed that will not be known or brought out into the open." (Luke 8:17)

Living where you work creates some interesting scenarios. For instance, I remember watching a crime television show one evening, thinking I was alone in the priest section of the rectory/office, when a voice behind me said, "I'm not sure you should be watching that show Father. There are is a lot of murders in it."

At first thinking it might be the voice of the Lord or perhaps the Bishop had a surveillance camera installed and was observing my television show selection, then I realized it was a parishioner coming from the Church office within the rectory, who had wandered into our living quarters.

Or the time I came down the stairs only to hear the parish volunteer secretary say to an innocent caller on the phone, "Oh, I heard the water stop in the bathroom upstairs...I'll bet if we wait a moment, Father will be right down."

When I was instructed in the seminary that the Church was my spouse, I really didn't realize what they were saying! But of the many roles my spouse has asked me to do, the one role I find I am most ill equipped for, is being a security guard.

"Unless the Lord watches over the city, the watchman stays awake in vain." (Psalm 127:1)

Parish buildings are similar to castles, but instead of surrounded by moats, we are surrounded by parking lots. A lot happens in our moat, or parking lots. They are gathering spaces for both teenagers and police officers. Recreational places for hockey, skateboarders, and rock climbers. Yes, the rock climbers see the church not as a place of worship, but taking after the example of Moses, a mountain to climb! They are also places of meetings. Here is where the "meeting after the meeting" occurs: where the real business of the church happens.

As a young associate, I was often sent out on patrol of the parking lot just to make certain all was well, and all was in its place. I was also able to do much "parking lot ministry." People were more relaxed and I was more approachable in the parking lot, rather than making an appointment with me in a stuffy parish office with lots of religious art looking at you.

As a pastor or director of the retreat center, I continued my tours of the parking lot and surrounding grounds of our castle. On patrol one dark evening, I noticed as I looked outside my bedroom window a car pull up. Often people will circle the retreat center and get themselves into a dead end where the food trucks unload. Thinking this was the case, I was surprised to see the car remain parked next to the dumpster with its lights on.

"Great," I thought. "Probably someone is dumping a filthy mattress or 1970's earth tone sofa into our dumpster!"

It is not unusual for people to use a church's dumpster for large items such as soiled mattresses, cigarette scented sofas and chairs, or worse, used diapers. Sometimes people dump their cars in the parking lot, or set a mattress on fire. Hence the need for the resident pastor to assume the role of security guard.

I could not hear any noise from the dumpster lid being opened, so I assumed the parked car with its lights on was another matter: this being young lovers. Why young lovers would pick the parking lot of a church to discourse on matters of intimate passion I cannot begin to understand, but I have interrupted more than one couple in the midst of their "conversation" in a church parking lot. Perhaps I should use such opportunities to teach the insights of the "Theology of the Body" but mostly I use it as an opportunity to preach the insightful lesson of the young man in Mark's Gospel (Mark 14:51) who ran away not fully clothed.

Not wanting to, but knowing it was necessary, I slipped on my priestly slippers. (The alternative slippers are my bunny slippers...not really manly enough for security detail.)

Putting on my coat but allowing my black and white collar to be visible, I slowly approached the parked car with its lights still on. It is amazing how the little bit of white on my clerical collar in such situations will radiate like the moonlight in the nocturnal darkness.

In the shadows, I could see a very large man. Not wanting to startle him because I could not figure out what he was doing, and due to his very large size, I quietly cleared my throat.

He acted as if he was a deer. Hearing me, he froze. Didn't move an inch. Now I was worried, so I quietly said, "Is everything alright?"

Turning towards me, I realized he was standing with one leg in the air. One leg was clothed with a dress pant leg, the other was not. He was in the midst of putting on pants. Standing with one leg in the pants, the other out and in his white tee shirt, he said, "Oh my Gosh! You startled me!"

"What's going one," I mildly asked, still not understanding what was happening, but trying to act like I was not seeing anything unusual.

"Oh, I was on my way out of town and just got off work, so I thought I would quickly change out of my suit and get into more comfortable clothes. I've got to travel a long ways tonight." He explained.

Not wanting to have further conversation with a half dressed man next to a trash can in my parking lot, I quickly said, "Okay. Well drive safely." And made a quick exodus back into my residence, priestly slippers and all.

Once back in the house, I saw the car lights slowly turning and leaving the parking lot. Chuckling to myself, I realized what had happened. Here an innocent man was trying to find a quiet, out the way, dark place to simply change out of his work clothes into comfortable driving clothes. He ducks into what he perceives as a dark dead end road behind a large building that seems vacant.

What he didn't realize is the obscure out of the way road he chose was visible to twenty-three retired priests who rarely miss any activity out their windows and a retreat center director who was on high alert. Not only that, but he was in direct line of sight of the Bishop's residence! The poor man would have been less noticed in the parking lot of a grocery store in broad daylight!

A priest takes on many roles, just like a parent. A security guard yes, but even better, as I reflected on this experience, I put on my hat of a philosopher.

"Nothing in all creation is hidden from God's sight. Everything is uncovered and lay bare before the eyes of him to whom we must give account." (Hebrews 4:13)

How many times have I tried to find that obscure out of the way road, thinking my desires or actions would not be of concern to anyone but me, only to realize nothing is truly hidden from Him. How many times have I acted in an unchristian like manner because I thought I was anonymous?

Jesus said it well, *"You are the light of the world. A city on a mountain cannot be hidden...just so, your light must shine before others, that they may see your good deeds and glorify your heavenly Father."* (Matthew 5:14-16)

2 ITS HARD BEING A CELEBRITY

"Then the women said to Naomi, "Blessed is the Lord who has not failed to provide you today with a redeemer. May he become famous in Israel!" Ruth 4:14

It happened again. I met a person whose face lit up when I introduced myself. "Oh, you're the one who writes those articles in the Catholic newspaper! Oh I love those articles!"

"Well, yes, I am," I reply. This then causes a cascade of thoughts: 'What did I say or do before they recognized me?......Did I embarrass myself by doing something stupid or acting grumpy?...I'll bet they are disappointed to find out I am real and really not as all together as my articles make me seem.'

Being a celebrity is hard work. You have to be "acting" all the time. Acting like you have it all together. Acting like you have insightful answers always. Always trying to be what you think others think of you. It can be both dangerous and tiring.

But Rita taught me otherwise. Born in 1919, I met Rita and her husband when she was in her mid-70's. She was a faithful Catholic. Her husband was a faithful non-Catholic. I mean, he was always at Mass, even many weekdays, raised his children Catholic, and a very good Christian man. But never entered the Catholic Church sacramentally. He was a faithful non-Catholic Catholic.

Rita was like Saint Monica. Always praying and inviting her husband to the Catholic faith. Respectfully, he declined. But this never deterred Rita. She continued to pray, pray, and invite. I guess you could call it "reverently nagging." Soon I would play a part in the invitation.

Rita frequently asked me what she could do to get her husband to join the Church. I told her what she was already doing: pray and invite. But eventually he became ill with a heart condition. Invited over to the house, I entered the room where he was sitting. I could tell things had changed for him. Both physically and spiritually.

Rita had already prepped me. "I think he is ready!" she told me. Ready to enter the Church I knew she meant. So, upon entering the room, I simply asked: "Well, what do you think about getting baptized?" "Sure," he replied. It was really that simple!

The next week, we gathered at the Church and he was baptized. Rita outshone the sun, so great was her beam! It was a simple ceremony of Baptism, Confirmation, and First Communion. I don't remember how long, but Rita's husband lived for some time afterwards, faithfully receiving the sacraments next to his beaming wife. Finally he entered into eternal life. Well prepared and with his wife at his bed side.

End of story? Not even close! So who got the credit for this conversion? Rita? ....No. Our Lord?....No. Saint Monica?....Nope. Me! I got all the credit!

What did I do? Nothing! I simply came when summoned. Rita did all the evangelization. The Lord softened the heart and created the circumstances. All I did was be a priest. Pretty simple, but from that day onward, I walked on water in Rita's eyes. I was her celebrity.

So when I entered Rita's room, seeing she was close to joining her husband, I knew she would want to see me. Bolting up in bed, something she had not done for days, and with a strong voice, "Well, there he is! Father Ken! "

What an animated reception! Then Rita, for the umpteenth time related how I, Father Ken, brought her husband into the Church, baptizing him. How grateful she was for all I did! Embarrassed, I knew better than to correct a dying woman how I had little to do with her husband's conversion. It was the Lord and her persistent prayer and invitation, not me! After giving her the Commendation of the Dying, I left. She passed from this life to her husband and the Lord a few hours later.

Rita saw in me what I don't see in myself. She saw the workings of the Lord. I see in myself the inability to be what I think others want me to be. She saw in me Christ. Something I don't always see in my mirror.

Scripture reminds us, "The Lord delights in those who fear Him, who put their hope in His unfailing love." Psalm 147:11

I think of Rita when people see me and recognize me as "That priest who writes those stories," or "The priest who baptized my child," or "The priest who was there at the bedside of my wife." I remember it's not me who they are seeing, even if they make a fuss over me. It is the Lord they recognize.

"In persona Christi: at the moment of priestly Ordination, the Church has also made this reality of "new clothes" visible and comprehensible to us externally through being clothed in liturgical vestments. In this external gesture she wants to make the interior event visible to us, as well as our task which stems from it: putting on Christ; giving ourselves to him as he gave himself to us." Pope Benedict at the Holy Chrism Mass homily, 2007.

The greeting Our Heavenly Father will give us in eternal life, I suspect, will be similar to Rita's greeting. He sees us as a celebrity. He will see in us what we don't see in ourselves. Goodness. Faith. And most of all, His Son, Jesus.

Being a celebrity doesn't have to be hard work. You don't have to act like you have it all together or be insightful, or try to be what you think others think of you. Nope, all we have to do is be ourselves, and the Lord will take care of the rest. Sometimes smoothing our rough edges, and often placing us where we need to be at the right time.

Thank you Rita for loving me as our Heavenly Father loves me. A great reminder.

3 ACTUALLY, REALLY, AND AHHH, LIKE!

"The glory of the young is their strength, and the dignity of the old is gray hair." Proverbs 20:29

Virtue is not instantly instilled in a priest or a Christian's life. A virtue is the habitual and firm disposition to do good, according to the Catholic Catechism, (CCC #1803) however before virtuous habits are a natural part of one's life, one goes through maturing and even some silliness. Perhaps even a lot of silliness.

"Ahh,…" he said. He was a professor in our seminary. A kind man in his late sixties who was teaching us the beauty of the Blessed Virgin Mary and how her fiat, or yes, allowed us to participate in the salvation of Jesus Christ.

"Ahh, Mary was, ahh, the , ahh, new Eve. Ahh, her yes in the new garden of Eden, ahh, allowed us to say, ahh, our yes." He lectured. He was a very good teacher and writer, but had developed a bad habit of when forming his sentences, pausing and thinking of what he wanted to say next, he would use the word "ahh,' to fill in the gap.

Being the mature seminarians that we were, virtuous in our ways; we of course, ignored this little annoying habit and focused on the truths and goodness being taught.....did I mention virtuous habits are learned and not instantaneous?

Generally our beloved professor would use the word "ahhh," on average, once every minute and a half. We then were able to expect a piece of paper to be lifted casually by a virtuous seminarian at the front of the class about 45 minutes into the class with the number "100" on it. This meant our professor had reached the one hundredth "ahhh," and we were about half way through the class. (Yes, I've confessed my sin about this!)

We develop poor habits or overuse a word. It seems to go with society. "Ahh," or "huh?", and "like" can be overused words, especially among young people. "Like, ahh, well I think she like, will be there. But well, like, I'm not really, like sure." Responds a 7th grade girl when asked if her partner for serving will be in the sacristy waiting for us.

Today the overused word is "actually." Make a phone call to a company and ask for a particular person who is not there, and you get, "<u>Actually</u>, she is not here." Or "She <u>actually</u> is at lunch." Why are you telling me <u>actually</u>?

"Actually" means truth, or facts of a situation. It is also used to emphasize something someone has said or done is surprising. A good word, but overused. Tomorrow, another word will take its place, but actually today, "actually" is the THE word. And actually it is a theological word at that!

What are some things we "actually" believe? The Real Presence. We believe the bread and wine actually becomes the body, blood, soul, humanity and divinity of Jesus Christ. Really and actually. What a wondrous gift we have in the Eucharist. The actual presence of God!

The Resurrection. In giving children tours of the diocesan retreat center, I make it a point to lead them down the hall of the Apostle statues. Replicas of the statues which adorn Saint Peter's Basilica in Rome, although a lot smaller.

I like to bring the children, especially 6th graders to the statue of St. Bartholomew. The statues depict the apostles with the instruments of their martyrdom. St. Bartholomew was skinned alive so his statue displays his skin folded over his arm with the impression of his face on the skin. Quite gruesome.

Sixth graders are at the point where they are young enough to be awed but such gruesome displays, but old enough to understand the implications. In showing them the Apostles, especially Bartholomew, I ask the question: "If Jesus didn't really rise from the dead, surely after one swipe of skin, Bartholomew would have cried out, 'Just kidding!'"

Walking from statue to statue, the children begin to realize the different ways the Apostles died. Crucifixion, beheading, sawed, etc. None of the Apostles lived an easy life, nor were their deaths easy.

Prior to the priesthood, priests had lives. Real, actual lives. We had friends, even girlfriends; and we had jobs. Some had careers and some just summer jobs between semesters. During college and the seminary, I worked at a beer delivery company. I remember well the first time one of the drivers found out I was studying to be a priest.

"Really?" he asked, "You are really going to be a priest?" I assured him I was just in the process of finding out, of formation, but that did not deter his incredulous response. Then came the real or "actual" question: "You know you can't get married, don't you?"

Acting like it was the first time I heard of this requirement, I replied, "Actually do you think they would ask me to do that???" Yes, actually they would. They actually did.

Perhaps this over used word best describes the faith of the Apostles, and ours. Actually! Meaning the truth or the facts of the situation. And more importantly meaning to emphasize something someone has said or done is surprising.

My coworker was surprised I was willing to be a celibate priest. Today, society is just as surprised the Church teaches marriage is between a man and woman.

Jesus said, "I am the Bread of Life. If you believe in me, you will have eternal life."(John 6:35) Even when faced with the actual reality of the risen Jesus the disciples are still doubtful, so impossible did the thing seem.

"And while they were telling these things, He Himself stood in their midst. But they were startled and frightened and thought they were seeing a spirit. And He said to them, "Why are you troubled, and why do doubts arise in your hearts? See My hands and My feet, that it is I Myself; touch Me and see, for a spirit does not have flesh and bones as you see that I have." [And when He had said this, He showed them His hands and His feet.]" Luke 24:36-43

So, if you feel like your faith is not strong enough or virtuous enough, remember, virtue is not instantly instilled in a priest or a Christian's life. Actually it takes a life time...and like, actually, God is patient with us! Actually!

4 FOLLOWING BEHIND

"When the Lord saw that he (Moses) had turned aside to look, God called out to him from the bush: Moses! Moses! He answered, "Here I am." Exodus 3:4.

We priests call each other brothers. As a diocesan priest I do not live in community. I live in a fraternity. A community of priests would literally live under the same roof. But a fraternity of priests especially as diocesan priests we live separately and yet we are all brothers.

One of the great joys of the priest is to live with other priests. One of the most challenging things for priest to do is to live with other priests. Living with other priests we experience both the positive things about them but also the things that drive us crazy.

Coming down the stairs one morning at the rectory I was surprised to see a parishioner in my living room. The other priest I lived with had an appointment at 6:30 in the morning. And the parishioner was waiting for him. The priest I lived with often would take appointments until nine or 10 o'clock at night too.

At first I thought this is what being a priest was. Then I soon realized that I could never keep up with this man who is 20 years my senior. I remember being very frustrated saying, "If this is what being a priest is, I don't think I can do it."

My brother priest was very gentle with me. His style of priesthood and personality was that of the Energizer Bunny. Where mine was more of a tortoise. I soon came to realize I needed to be myself and to live the priesthood according to my personality and gifts.

But being a brother priest and calling each other "brothers" is very accurate. Just like in a family where brothers might drive each other crazy, they also support one another.

My blood brother loves to hike he lives in Colorado. And I go out to visit and to go hiking with him in the mountains. Now there are two ways to hike in the mountains. One way is to go as fast as you can and as far as you can. This is what I call endurance hiking. Hiking for exercise.

The other way you can hike in the mountains is what I call the lollygagging way. It's the way I like to hike. It's a manner of hiking where you can stop and smell the roses. Take a picture of a beautiful scene. And most of all catch your breath in the high altitude!

When I hike with my brother in the mountains he has learned to allow me to hike first. Otherwise, he far outdistances me and I get lost.

When you are hiking in the mountains or in some unfamiliar territory it is easier to follow someone. This way you know exactly where you're going and as long as you keep them in sight, you feel safe and secure. I have found as a priest my walk with the Lord is similar. Rarely does the Lord take the lead.

Another way of hiking is to walk side-by-side with someone, however this can be awkward and difficult. It's hard to match another person's stride. Sometimes they're taller and faster or shorter and slower. Then at times you might decide to go to the left and your partner who is walking beside you will go to the right. Then there's a problem.

In my priesthood I can see that the Lord doesn't walk beside me either.

Finally when you're walking in the mountains or in unfamiliar territory you can walk with the person behind you. This is what my brother does. Behind me he tells me which direction I need to go. Sometimes it's kind of scary because I know that I am first, walking through cobwebs or branches, and sometimes I feel like bear bait. It's kind of scary.

In my priesthood, this is how I have learned to walk with The Lord and with my brother priests.

The prophet Isaiah wrote in Isaiah 30 "While from behind a voice shall sound in your ears, 'this is the way walk it when you should turn to the right or to the left.'"

I would much rather for the Lord or for my brother priest just tell me what to do. And to lead me where I can see them at all times. However our Lord honors our free will and all he wants to do is to influence us. He can do this best by always being behind us. Always there to support us, and gently guiding us from behind.

As a middle-aged priest now I realize how many of my brother priests have done just that for me. At times I wish they would just lead and tell me what to do. But they to honor my free will. My choices. Even my personality.

Priest called each other brothers, because like brothers we sometimes compare ourselves to one another. Compete with one another. Even complain about one another. Like the Lord in Isaiah 30, my brother priests are a voice from behind always supporting and gently guiding me.

Whose voice is guiding you? Who are you guiding gently from behind with your voice?

5 PRIESTS AND THEIR DOGS

Qui me amat, amat e canem meam

"When the young man left home, accompanied by the angel, the dog followed Tobiah out and went along with them." Tobit 6:2

There he was. Staring out the window of the car. Intently looking at the doors of the local grocery store. Such intensity I rarely see.

I wondered what was going on. What would cause him to be so still? Stare so attentively. Nothing would move his gaze off the doors of the store. No distraction of people coming or going. Not even I looking at him staring disturbed his gaze to the entrance.

"He" was a golden retriever dog. He was intently watching the doors of the grocery store open and close as the customers came and went. As a dog owner, I comprehended what was going on. His master was shopping, and the retriever was waiting expectantly for the masters return. Nothing was going to distract him from his gaze.

There has been a recent phenomenon in the church as of late. I've noticed an increased number of priests who own dogs. It is a good thing I believe. The care of a dog gives a priest, who often lives alone, another being to care for and to give attention. The attention a dog gives to his master is unparalleled.

Having had a dog, it always bothered me when people would equate my dog to being my child. They would talk to the dog and ask him about his "daddy." I often would unsuccessfully refrain from sarcastically telling them his "daddy" was a lot shaggier than I. They were understanding, however, of the bond between a dog and his owner. Sometimes this bond is embarrassing. I remember a brother priest frustrated with me told me I paid more attention to the dog than him. He was probably right. The dog needed more attention than him, but it did help me realize my brother priest needed it too.

Brother priests seem to fall into one of three categories when it comes to dogs. They either love dogs. Hate dogs. And then there is the final category: The priest who grew up on the farm. They act like the dog is livestock, looking at you like you are crazy to have a cow in the house!

A dog changes a person though. The constant attention it gives its master can only soften the most hardened hearts. I think of one priest in particular. A farm boy who served the church for over 60 years as a priest. A sometimes gruff, absolutely no nonsense priest, frugal to a fault. What a surprise to see beside his lamp next to his bed, a picture of his old coon dog. A dog that passed on probably 40 years previously. Even the most hardened heart softens.

Such relationships are important for a shepherd to experience. C.S. Lewis wrote in *The Four Loves*, *"To love at all is to be vulnerable. Love anything and your heart will be wrung and possibly broken. If you want to make sure of keeping it intact you must give it to no one, not even an animal. Wrap it carefully round with hobbies and little luxuries; avoid all entanglements. Lock it up safe in the casket or coffin of your selfishness. But in that casket, safe, dark, motionless, airless, it will change. It will not be broken; it will become unbreakable, impenetrable, irredeemable. To love is to be vulnerable."*

He continued to stare out the window. You could tell by his rapid attention to anything that moved, he was waiting, and ready to move excitedly when called upon. Nothing would keep his gaze from the horizon.... *"But while he was still a long way off, his father saw him and was filled with compassion for him; he ran to his son, threw his arms around him and kissed him."* (Luke 15:20) "He" was the father of the prodigal son.

An interesting phenomenon. Priests getting dogs. How often do we as priests sit in the confessional, watching and waiting for the prodigal to return? How often as parents? Grandparents, aunts or uncles wait for the prodigal? How often does our Lord wait for us?

There is a painting of the return of the Prodigal Son by Bartolome Esteban Murillo (1667-70) depicting the father welcoming the son. When I look at the painting, I don't see the father as representing God the Father, rather Murillo also has a little white terrier dog, jumping up at the legs of the Prodigal Son with his tail wagging.

I can hear the thoughts of that dog: "Oh boy! Finally you are home! I've been waiting for you! Tell me where you have been and then let's play! Oh boy! You're finally home!!!"

"Blessed are those servants whom the master will find on the alert when he comes; truly I say to you, that he will gird himself to serve, and have them recline at the table, and will come up and wait on them." (Luke 12:13)

A priest can learn a lot from a dog!

6 SERVING CHRIST IN ORDINARY WAYS

"Observing the boldness of Peter and John and perceiving them to be uneducated, ordinary men, they were amazed, and they recognized them as companions of Jesus." Acts 4:13

Generally when I arrive, I rearrange the chairs so a person seated behind me can speak into my ear unseen. Or a person can sit in front of me and face to face, experiencing the forgiveness the Lord wishes to offer in the Sacrament of Confession at a parish penance service.

The chair behind me, I prefer to sit in a manner where I can best hear the penitent. If they choose to be anonymous, often they will whisper in an inaudible whisper, requiring me to lean back farther in my chair to understand them.

The chair in front, I place two leg's length before me at a comfortable distance. Inevitably the chair seems to germinate more than its' four legs, and slowly creeps closer to me, only to have me push it back to its proper place when a penitent leaves. I like some distance between us. That whole personal space thing.

Recently I was driving to a parish penance service. Skipping the dinner beforehand knowing from experience there is nothing worse than eating a famously hefty meal, then sitting in a confessional for two hours.

As I was driving, listening to the Bible, a great way to meditate while driving, I was listening about the separation of the sheep from the goats at the last judgment (Matthew 25:31-46). A passage which describes the spiritual and corporeal works of mercy: "For I was hungry and you gave me food..." A passage I often use to explain that stewardship is the sharing of our gifts and being of Christ to one another. A passage which I often am uncomfortable hearing.

It might seem odd to you I find this passage so difficult to hear, but as I hear the words I am reminded and challenged. Wondering what group I belong.

I consider the manager of a local food diner for those in need, and how I am often asked, "Hey Father, we would love to see you helping us?" Or I remember the years I assisted in completing paperwork for an organization helping people stay in their homes and out of homeless shelters. As much as I would like, I cannot any longer give even an afternoon a week for such a worthy cause.

But I am a priest, not ordained to serve a computer screen! How can I not assist the poor, the hungry, the homeless? What kind of preacher am I who cannot even take an afternoon out of a week and serve the poor? All my needs are taken care of by the Church. How can I be so selfish?

The more I considered the passage the more uncomfortable I became, thinking about priests who go to Haiti or Mexico to build houses or distribute medicine, I thought maybe I could do something like that. No, I can't hammer nails straight, and I only speak English. Why couldn't I be a better priest?

With all of these thoughts ruminating within me, I sulked through the Penance Service, not wanting to fully participate. Not feeling worthy.

Going to my assigned place, I rearranged the chairs in my usual way. As I put my weight down into the chair, a cushy chair provided, for we wouldn't want Father not be comfortable, my first penitent arrived.

As expected upon arrival, up comes the chair so close to me they could hold my hands. I recoiled into my cushy chair trying to establish some personal space. Leaning forward towards me, negating any personal space I established, they said: "Father, I like to go to confession face to face if that's alright. I love coming to confession face to face, because then I can see the face of Christ who forgives my sins."

Like lightning out of a blue sky, God shook me. This is how I am to be Christ. Feeding the hungry, sheltering the homeless, and the other works of mercy are vital, but I have been called to be in persona Christi, in the person of Christ through the gifts of the priesthood: forgiving sins, consecrating the bread and wine into the Body and Blood of Christ, proclaiming the Good News of the Gospel. This penitent is the Christ I am to serve.

The mere fact I was driving to another town to hear confessions is missionary work, albeit not Haiti or Mexico, but just as vital. Just being who I am and doing what I do is enough, if I do it as Christ would.

I suspect many a parent, grandparent, teacher, police officer, or anyone who serves others understood this long ago. Feeding the hungry and sheltering the homeless is serving the person in need right in front of you with the gifts given. And that person might even be your son or daughter, or parishioner.

We don't have to travel across the world to serve Christ. We can serve Christ in our ordinary lives in seemingly ordinary ways.

7 THE TURTLE BRIGADE

"Even to your old age I am he, even when your hair is gray I will carry you; I have done this, and I will lift you up, I will carry you to safety." Isaiah 46:4

I had just completed Sunday Mass at a parish. I provide substitute help for priests and pastors who are away from their parishes. I don't ask where they are going. But boy do their parishioners ask me!

Generally the first question I am asked when I arrive at a parish to substitute is, "Where's Father?" When I give my standard reply of, "I didn't ask.", I often get a downcast answer of, "Well, he didn't tell me either." And then they proceed to tell me where he might be.

Even if I do know where the pastor is, I try to avoid telling because then they ask: "Why is he going there?" Or "He doesn't have family there does he?" We truly are "fathers" to our parishioners. No different from the children of a family, curious to know where mom or dad is when they are absent.

After Mass, no matter what parish, whether it is a large parish of thousands, or a small parish of fifteen, the after Mass on-slaught is the same. I generally try to stand a little out of the way, but in a central place to greet the parishioners as they leave. In doing so, I understand a little bit better when the Gospel writers speak of Jesus being "crushed by the crowd." (Luke 8:42)

People leaving Mass fall into several categories:

The "*Got to get to Father*" category. This well-meaning person bee-lines it for Father after every Mass. Not necessarily to wish a good day, but because they have a question or a comment if fully addressed

by the priest, would last well into the Sunday afternoon golf games on television. (By the way, these Sunday afternoon golf games on television is the manner in which God cast Adam into a deep slumber – Genesis 2:21, a little known fact!)

Then there is *"The Hugger,"* pushing past your outstretched hand for a hand shake, only satisfied with a great big bear hug. Somewhat reminds of the women who wanted to touch Jesus. (Mark 5: 21-34) Generally this person is one extreme or another. Either a precious small child hugging your knees, or a huge calloused farmer in overalls whose embrace encompasses as you would imagine God the Father embracing you.

Every Sunday there is also *"The Complimenter."* They always have a pleasant expression on their face, warmly greet you, and tell you what a wonderful message you gave in the homily, even if it was your associate priest who gave the homily. I've learned to be suspicious of this person. They seem to be born with the gift to get a message out of the homily. Any homily. I think I could read from the phone book, and they would still compliment me. Perhaps they are really giving thanks to the Holy Spirit, and I am just the instrument....nah, it's all about me!

Then comes *"The Complainer."* The music is too loud, too soft, too 1970's, too conservative. Or they couldn't hear the priest, couldn't see the priest, and couldn't understand the priest. Or you get, "Father so and so, he gets us out in less than 50 minutes." I wish The Complainer was before The Complimenter, but it never seems in that order. Maybe this is the Holy Spirits way of telling me, it's really not all about me!

Finally, there is *"The Turtle Brigade."* These are probably the most important and special in God's eyes and a pastor's eye too.

These are the parishioners who are in wheel chairs or who use walkers. Like a herd of turtles, they have patiently waited for the rabbits of the congregation to leave, and they slowly but deliberately make their way to greet Father.

Her name was 98 year old Ruth. She had outlived both family and friends. I often heard her say, "I think God forgot me!" Generally toward the ends of the brigade of walkers, canes, and wheelchairs, she always patiently waited her turn to greet me.

With a pleasant smile, in the midst of her obvious pain and discomfort, never a negative word on her lips. Her greeting was the same, "It is good to see you Father. Thank you for Mass!" Then she would tell me about the news of the neighborhood or some tidbit she had pick up from the Meals on Wheels volunteer who visited her home.

The sending forth of Mass includes many walks of life with the parish life. It really is a procession from the earthly heavenly liturgy to God's Kingdom. After one particular slow procession after Mass, I knew it might be the last one for Ruth.

That week, I was called to Ruth's home. She was in the process of processing to her real home. God remembered. Immediately coming into her bedroom, the same smile greeted me and the same warm greeting, "Oh Father, it is so good to see you!" It was as if she was greeting me after Mass, not on her death bed.

"Oh you didn't have to come Father, but I'm so glad you did!" Ruth said. After praying the prayers of accommodation for the dying, she slipped into a deep sleep. I knew she would soon begin her last process from this earthly liturgy to the Heavenly Liturgy, this time without a walker.

I can imagine what Ruth said to the Lord later that day when she completed her procession home. "Oh Father! It is so good to see you God my Father. Thank you for the Mass! Thank you for my life!" I hope I leave this world the way Ruth left Sunday Mass and this world: with appreciation and gratitude.

But perhaps we must go through the stage of the rabbit before we can fully embrace the process of the turtles.

"[Jesus said to Peter] Amen, amen, I say to you, when you were younger, you used to dress yourself and go where you wanted; but when you grow old, you will stretch out your hands, and someone else will dress you and lead you where you do not want to go." He said this signifying by what kind of death he would glorify God. And when he had said this, he said to him, "Follow me." John 21: 18-19

I wish we all could be in Ruth's category leaving Mass and this world.

8 BORDOM, MISCHIEVOUSNESS, AND OPPORTUNITY

"For idleness teaches much mischief." Book of Sirach 33:29

Sometimes people ask me if priests get lonely. 'No more than anyone else,' I generally respond. As diocesan priests, we live solitary lives. But it didn't begin that way.

I remember standing in my dorm room at the Seminary. For the first several years we would share a room with a brother seminarian. Having grown up with an older brother, I was not unaccustomed to sharing a room, but in the seminary, the brother I shared a room with was not from my family, but from another part of the country.

My first roommate was from Vermont. A large man whose voice reminded me of Paul Bunyan. He was as scared and bewildered as I was to be in a seminary, far from home. Being the shorter and smaller of the two, I took the top bunk in self-defense.

I had never slept in bunk beds and was somewhat afraid the bunk might not hold my roommate from Vermont, and the bed would come crashing down upon me during the night. I could imagine the seminary rector calling my mother, telling her son that he was crushed by a falling seminarian! Having enough fears of a new studies, new place, new life, I thought the least I could do is make the climb to the upper bunk for the night's rest.

Those years of having a roommate were at times difficult. Such as roommates who walked in their sleep, climbing onto the window sill of the fifth story building to talk to people who weren't there; or the roommate who decorated the room with thousands of relics of saints, parallel only to the catacombs of Rome. Or the roommate who thought the dorm room was a gymnasium, bouncing basketballs off the walls.

Later as a young priest I learned the combination of boredom, mischievousness, and opportunity was a dangerous mix. Such as the time a person riding on a bus filled with teenagers would fall asleep, only to find his face was covered with lipstick, rouge, and fingernails with matching color. I still refuse to fall asleep on a bus!

Perhaps seminarians are simply older teenagers because the same combination of boredom, mischievousness, and opportunity abound in the seminary, causing similar results. Especially among roommates.

Whenever a seminarian would leave for a long weekend, it was not certain what he would find upon returning to his room. Such as the seminarian who returned to his room late Sunday night, only to find everything in his room gift wrapped in newspaper. When I say everything, I mean everything! Every book. Every picture. Every pencil. Every pen. Even the toothbrush!

The amount of time it took to carefully wrap all the items, the amount of paper and tape, not to mention the energy it took. All going to show how that seminarian later would be a whiz of organizing a parish after being able to organize and inspire so many of his brothers to assist him in this task. Organizing a parish dinner would be a walk in the park for him.

Or the seminarian roommate who decided to redecorate his roommates room by rearranging the furniture. He did so in the exact opposite manner. A mirror image of what it was. Talk about being disorientated! Coming home from a long weekend in the parish, the seminarian thought he was in the wrong room, and kept looking to see where he was moved before realizing what happened.

But seminary professors are not immune from the effects of boredom, mischievousness, and opportunity. I remember on a particular slow Sunday, coming down the hall of the seminary bumping to a long line of men carrying a desk, chair, a file cabinet, and typewriter (this was before computers!).

"Where are you going with all this stuff?," I asked,

"The elevator, of course." One of them replied. 'Of course,' I thought, 'how dumb of me to ask!'

Following them, I watched with interest how they replicated the office of one of our professors in the elevator: desk, chair, cabinet. Even a lamp! Up and down, up and down it went, until the professor came home to find his office in perpetual motion. That was when the rector, the priest in charge of the seminary, went into motion who didn't seem to appreciate the rising and falling office.

Even the saints were not immune to participate in the mischief. When you purchase statues for a seminary, one really should purchase the statues of marble, not plaster or plastic. Marble is generally immoveable. Plaster and plastic is transportable. When you purchase plaster or plastic statues then finding St. John or St. Therese hiding behind your door in your dorm room, or getting on the elevator with Saint John the Baptist dressed up with muffs, scarf, and a hat were not that uncommon.

Boredom, mischievousness, and opportunity. A deadly combination especially with roommates, but those memories are the memories that last a lifetime and bring a smile while I live alone now... at least until the next priest convocation! A great time of "boredom, mischievousness, and opportunity!"

9 CONTEMPLATIVE PRAYER AND DISTRACTIONS

"Be still and know that I am God..." Psalm 46:10

Contemplative prayer is not difficult. I think the enemy introduces the concept in our minds that contemplation is difficult. "Only for saints", we think, so we will not try it and receive the wonderful benefits it gives.

Saint Teresa of Avila wrote the Lord makes everything easy for the person who really loves, "Beyond all natural reason, You make things so possible that You manifest clearly there's no need for anything more than truly to love You..."

I have been taught, to excel quickly and deeply in prayer life, it is important to simply be in the presence of the Lord and love. Contemplative prayer simply loves. When I teach this to others, I use several analogies, such as a tabernacle light before the tabernacle. What does it do? It simply is "present" to the "Presence."

Or if the person I am teaching is a dog owner, this is one of the greatest examples of contemplative prayer. If you have or ever had a dog as a pet, you will understand. When you are with your pet dog, much of his time, he is simply watching you, wanting to be in your presence.

Go to another room, and soon enough, a wet nose will poke its way through the door way. Sometimes he will remain in the room, and sometimes just checking to make certain you are still there. When he does remain in the room, what does he do? He humbly watches you.

Yes, I know, he is probably thinking, "When will he go to the refrigerator? Food...food, food." But even a dog understands his master is the one responsible for him, and feeds him. If only we understand our Lord is our master, is responsible for us, and feeds us. Then we would advance greatly in prayer!

Armed with this great knowledge, I entered the parish church early one morning before the Sunday Mass. Settling in the pew, I decided I would try to be simply "present to the Presence," like a dog before his Master, just attentive.

Quickly words left me, and I was observant of the Lord's Presence. I had no words to say, not woes to give, no petitions to recite. I was present to Him. It really was easy, but that's when it happened.

At first I was surprised, then overwhelmed. It was a simple sound. Perhaps I was mistaken. Perhaps it was in my head. Could this really be happening? Would God really allow this to happen to me? Why me? What did I do to deserve this?

CLICK! There I heard it again. What could the Lord be saying to me? CLICK! Was this a spiritual phenomenon? CLICK! Perhaps it was a type of Morse code from the angels. CLICK!

By now, I was curious. No longer fully present to the Lord, I looked around. Only a few people were in the church. The ushers were claiming their rightful places in the back of the church were they could stand through the Mass and point at their watches if my homily got too long for them. And the CYO was putting up tables in the foyer to sell their homemade cookies they purchased from the grocery store to earn money for their summer trip.

CLICK! There it was again. Now totally disengaged from the Lord's presence, I knew the sound was a familiar sound. Sorting out the different sounds in my memory, my mind went to different places I heard the sound. Slowly, eventually my intellect, a faculty of my spirit, sorted out the different places I heard this particular sound. CLICK!

No, surly not! But I guess He is found there too! His Presence is everywhere, so why not! Looking around the church once again, my sight settles on a married couple in the far corner of the church. CLICK! Yep, sure enough. The mystical sound was emanating from the woman. CLICK!

Settling back into my pew, I once more try to be present to the Presence. CLICK! But I know I am finished with my prayer time. CLICK!

Perhaps I am wrong. Contemplation IS difficult, only because it is so rewarding. For this reason the enemy tries to interrupt it with distractions. Realizing I cannot do anything about the woman in the church clipping her fingernails before Mass, my mind then goes to the obvious place...who is going to clean up all those clippings after Mass?

I then remember another saint, who got her name from Saint Teresa of Avila, that is, Saint Therese of Lisieux, and how she struggled in the chapel because of another nun who clattered her rosary beads against the pew, distracting her prayer.

I guess we all have our crosses in order to become saints! CLICK! CLICK! At least it wasn't her toe nails....I hope!

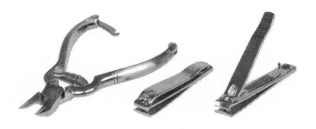

10 LITTLE GIRLS, BRIDES, GLITTER AND GRACE

"And the Lord their God will save them in that day. As the flock of His people; for they are as the stones of a crown, sparkling in His Land." The prophet Zechariah 9:16

I was unsure how to answer. As a priest, I am asked many things. "What happens after we die?" or "Did Jesus really understand His divinity when He was a child?" or even "Why do we call them Cardinals, these men who vote for a new pope? What does it all have to do with a bird at my birdfeeder?"

Most questions I can answer, although I'm not sure about the cardinal one. When I was a younger priest in my 20's or 30's, I had an answer for most things theologically. As I grow older, I don't....the grace of wisdom, age, and of being wrong too many times and humbled! Of course as a priest I can always fall back on the "it's a mystery!" answer, which often is really true.

A mystery is having some knowledge about a person or subject, but not a fullness of it. Such as to fully comprehend your spouse, friend, or family member, or oneself...it's a mystery. It's just not possible because of my limited ability to comprehend such knowledge. However the question I was asked, "It's a mystery!" answer would not suffice.

The person asking the question was a beautiful bride. Brides in of themselves are a mystery. How can such a beautiful, seemingly normal, and otherwise sane woman suddenly become such a different person when they are planning "my wedding?" It's a mystery how a bride will come to my parish office and say the words, "We just want a simple wedding," only to proceed to make an event as complicated as the Olympics.

A "simple wedding" means eight attendants instead of ten; a string quartet instead of an orchestra; and most of all, it means no complications, everything going smoothly. This of course means everyone agrees with one another....especially the priest.

There was the problem with my inability to answer. Thus far, I had negotiated with the bride the wedding would not include a little red wagon for the flower girl and ring bearer to ride down the aisle. We agreed not to have any Bon Jovi songs for the entrance of the bride. And we also agreed I would not wear pink vestments, even though pink would go nicely with the pastel colors she had picked for her spring wedding.

The sticking point in planning this "simple wedding" was glitter. Yes, glitter. This is a foreign substance created by a mischievous spirit wanting to create havoc in the lives of fathers of little girls, cleaning ladies, and parish priests. This clinging metallic substance liberally used on hair, dresses, and other such materials little girls wear is insidious and cunning. Just as soon as you think you have completely cleaned the church pews where middle

school girls sat transferring this stealthy substance to the seat of the pew, you realize it has multiplied in force to other pews.

My bride wanted the flower girls (yes, pleural... they multiplied) to abundantly toss glitter in the air as they processed before the bride and her father walking down the main aisle. The intended affect would be a glittery cloud from which the bride would pass through, finally reaching her prince awaiting at the end of the aisle.

Having already negotiated, well really commanded the absence of a red wagon, no Bon Jovi, and absolutely no priestly pink, I was feeling remorseful for the bride, who was truly a beautiful young Catholic woman who basically spent too much time watching the Bride's Channel and the Bachelor on television. And so I compromised. No throwing of glitter, but the children could throw glitter and blow bubbles at the couple outside in the couple's grand exit, forgetting after the" grand exit," the couple with all their glitter would make a less "grand entrance" into the church for pictures.

An hour after the "simple wedding," my volunteer wedding coordinator approached me while she was cleaning the church preparing it for the Saturday Vigil Mass.

"I thought you didn't allow glitter?" she said, "There is glitter all over the aisle and the pews. Everyone who sits there will have glitter on them. It will take forever to get rid of. How come you let them do that?" (And you thought I was in charge!)

"It's a mystery," I replied, meaning every word of it.

I wonder if God's grace is like glitter. Once a person has it, they transfer it to another. I hope the grace my young bride and her prince received at the wedding lasts forever and is transferred to others. Maybe I'll know how to answer next time I'm asked about glitter.

11 WE CAN LEARN A LOT FROM GOD'S CREATURES

"Whenever the living creatures give glory and honor and thanks to the one who sits on the throne, who lives forever and ever..." Book of Revelation 4:9

I wonder what he is thinking. He is so attentive. Occasionally he closes his eyes, and I can even tell when he is dreaming, but as soon as he awakes from his nap, he comes and finds me, and again plops down to watch me.

Even when I go to the deep recesses of the rectory where I do my deepest thinking and can see my true self in the mirror....come on, you know where I am talking about....even there; I can either hear a scratching on the door, or a cold wet nose poking itself through the crack.

I am talking, of course, about a dog.

You can learn a lot about God from a dog. In fact, you can learn a lot about God from all of nature and all of His living creatures.

"For he fashioned all things that they might have being, and the creatures of the world are wholesome; There is not a destructive drug among them nor any domain of Hades on earth..." Wisdom 4:1

While priests are not the first to realize this, our constant vision of seeking the Lord in all things, gives us new lenses. Have you noticed the number of priests who have dogs? Ever wonder why? Companionship? Sure. Comfort of another living being with you in the rectory? Sure. But most importantly, I think a dog, in fact all of nature, is a window into God, and I think God uses all things, including nature, to help us grow.

Pope Francis weighed into the debate as to whether dogs or any pet goes to heaven. In the December 11, 2014 New York Times edition it  was reported, "During a weekly general audience at the Vatican last month, the pope, speaking of the afterlife, appeared to suggest that animals could go to heaven, asserting, "Holy Scripture teaches us that the fulfillment of this wonderful design also affects everything around us."

It's really a silly question as to whether dogs go to heaven. (Of course they do!) Silly because heaven is so much more than earth, yet earth is a reflection of the goodness and magnanimous love of God.

Pope Francis gave a pastoral answer to a thorny theological question. But remember, theology is the study of God (theo = God, ology=study of). Therefore, studying His creation is studying Him.

Will His creation be in Heaven? It is a mystery, meaning, we do not have all the answers, but we have some. Scriptures are pretty explicit: Heaven is where God is all in all. A new heaven and a new earth. What will it all look like or mean? We will leave this up to the future, in the meantime, we can learn much from His creation.

For instance prayer. How to pray? Well, look at a

dog. We are his master. When a dog understands this, everyone is much happier. For about three years a dog goes through a puppy stage. This stage is where the dog is learning about the world, learning about self, learning who and what is his master. He gets into trouble often in this stage, but eventually he outgrows it. How? By accepting the human as his master, and then serving the human master by trying to please him. This is really all a dog wants to do, is to please his master.

Josh Billings, a humorist and lecturer is quoted as saying, "A dog is the only thing on earth that loves you more than he loves himself."

The analogy is obvious for us humans. We too go through a "puppy stage." Unfortunately it takes longer than three years for us. Sometimes, oftentimes, it takes a lifetime. We finally leave the puppy stage when we have the desire to please our Master above all things.

Even priests go through (or are going through) the puppy stage. The "puppy stage" of a priest is when he is more concerned about the delivery of his homily than the prayerful preparation before it. When he is more concerned about what people think about him, rather than about his love for them. When he puts his needs before others.

I remember well when I was (hopefully past tense) going through this stage. Worried so much about how the chalices and patens were placed in the cabinets of the sacristy, I completely missed the people who were in the sacristy. After one time, I realized I did not even acknowledge Barb who recently lost her husband. So worried about the "things" of the priesthood, I failed to see why I was really there. I now try to minister to people, not things.

A priest is at a disadvantage though. We don't have children. Many a time I've witnessed a selfish, reckless young pup of a boy become a mature and wise man because of his children. Bringing life into the world and putting the needs of this life before your own matures a man.

I would never want to equate a pet with a child, but for a priest our children (parishioners) go home at the end of Mass. They return to their lives as we to ours at the end of the day. Not so a father. And not so a pet owner, especially of a dog or puppy. No, as soon as we enter the rectory the dog needs something. Often attention. Attending to something or someone outside of oneself matures a man.

Yes, I often wonder what dogs think about when they watch their master. Is it love? Probably not, but I do know all a dog really wants is to be in his masters presence and to please his master. If only we could do the same. Yes, we can learn a lot from God's creatures. I hope my "pet teachers" are there to welcome me into heaven.

12 GRACE UNDER THE OAK TREE

"O Lord my God, I cried to you, and you have healed me." Psalm 30:2

Every month I would venture to Texas. Not for BBQ, football or longhorns. I would go to see Gertrude, on the street of Texas that is, in the state of Kansas.

Once a month I would park my car under the shade of a very old oak tree wondering how long the tree had maintained its vigor especially in the many drought stricken years we have experienced in Kansas. Once a month I would climb onto the porch, side stepping the many plants who were receiving their vitamin C from the sun. Once a month I would loudly rap at the door, then after a long couple of minutes see Gertrude sheepishly pull back the curtain and peep through the glass windowpane to see who was knocking at her door. It took her some time to get to the door because of her age and limitations.

Gertrude was in her mid-80's, living with her adult son. Both son and mother had experienced the devastating loss of a spouse. Now they shared not only the melancholy which comes with grief, but also a house. Most days they shared this space with grace, but some days they had to retreat to their own sections of the house, allowing the other room to find grace.

For over a year I meet with Gertrude on the first Friday of the month. I would minister the Anointing of the Sick and give her Holy Communion, offering also the opportunity to receive the Sacrament of Confession. She was eager to receive all the church had to offer. Most, if not all days, Gertrude was upbeat, hopeful of returning to her own home, and confident in the power of God in her life.

One particular First Friday, however, she was rather downcast. After inquiring what was de-pressing her spirit, she simply pulled up her pant leg, took off her shoe, and pointed to an open sore.

"It's been there for years," Gertrude said, "and I'm tired of it." The open sore was purplish and looked painful.

"It's been there for years!" I asked, "Then why haven't you said anything before?"

"Who wants to look at an old ladies sore foot!" she countered, "but today, it's really giving me fits. Can we pray over it?"

"I can do better than that," I responded, "let's ask Saint Peregrine to help."

In the year I had been seeing Gertrude, I would take a relic of Saint Peregrine mounted on a pewter crucifix and she would hold the relic while I anointed her and heard her confession. I could not remember if I explained to her the entire story of Peregrine, so with her open sore in mind, I described to her how Peregrine also had a sore and the manner in which he was healed.

Peregrine lived in Forli in the 13th Century. After a conversion experience he dedicated himself to the service of Our Lady as a member of the Servite Order. Peregrine had a love for penance and service of others in reparation of his sinful youth. By the time he was 60 years old, he was suffering from varicose veins which degenerated into cancer of the right leg.

His condition became critical. So critical the leg was to be amputated. The night before the operation Peregrine prayed before the crucifix. Either in a vision or a dream, Peregrine saw Jesus descend from the cross to heal his leg. The next day the surgeon arrived for the operation but could find no sign of cancer or even a wound.

Living another 20 years, Peregrine finally went home to the Lord in 1345 and since then has been seen as the patron of victims of cancer and other diseases.

I took the relic of St. Peregrine out of my sick call set but suddenly Gertrude grabbed the relic and pressed the pewter crucifix and relic onto the open sore. Quite surprised of her speed and quite squeamish of seeing my beautiful relic cross in the midst of her purplish sore, I began to pray the prayers from the Saint Peregrine devotional, and anointed her with the holy oil of the sick.

Many years ago, after losing a good friend to the disease of cancer, I asked the Lord for the gift of healing if it be His will. But I asked for this healing to be through the sacrament of the Anointing of the Sick. There have been times when the Lord granted my humble request, but more often than not, I saw spiritual healing but not physical healing.

Returning the next month, I had forgotten about the episode with the relic. Climbing onto the porch, amidst the potted flowers, underneath the shade of the oak tree, I didn't even get a chance to knock. The curtain was pulled back and I saw a very animated Gertrude peeking out. She had been sitting in a chair by the door, waiting for me. For how long, I can only imagine.

Throwing open the door, there she stood on one leg with the other leg protruding out. It was shoeless and sockless.

"Look!" she explained. Still not comprehending or remembering, I was amazed this 80'ish woman could stand on one leg. I kind of thought she might have lost it!

"Look at my foot! No sore! It's healed!" she cried out. Now remembering, I had her sit on the couch and I took a look. Sure enough, the sore was closed and although it was not completely healed, it was most certainly only a few days from being so.

"Saint Peregrine healed me!" Gertrude announced.

"It sure looks like it!" I agreed. And we begin to give prayers of thanks to God.

For several more years, I continued to visit Gertrude on First Fridays. Tenderly she would take the relic crucifix and kiss it when we prayed together. Eventually I was transferred to another parish and lost touch with Gertrude.

You can only imagine my surprise when some years later, at the new assignment, I was asked to come to the house of a woman parishioner whose mother had just moved in. It seems the mother's home had partially been burned down, and now was living with her daughter.

Entering the house, I was astounded to see Gertrude again. This time she was no longer able to answer the door, but from her bed, she encouraged me to pull a chair next to her bed.

"Did you bring it?" she asked with her eyes alight with fire. I knew exactly what she meant.

Digging into my sick call set, I handed her the relic crucifix. Lovingly she cupped it in her hands, and kissed it with such tenderness, bringing a tear to my eye.

"There's my old friend!" she reverently said.

Together we celebrated another year of First Fridays before Gertrude no longer needed to receive the sacraments on the First Friday of the month. In my heart, I am confident she was not only healed physically, but also strengthened spiritually, and is now experiencing the tender loving kiss of both Jesus and Peregrine.

I look forward to seeing her, my old friend, peeking around the curtains at the entrance of heaven. Not only was she healed and strengthened, but so was I.

For more information about Saint Peregrine, look up the National Shrine of Saint Peregrine in Chicago, IL at http://stperegrine.org/national-shrine/

13 HOPE

"They that hope in the Lord will renew their strength, they will soar on eagles' wings; They will run and not grow weary, walk and not grow faint." The prophet Isaiah 40:31

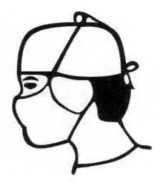 His disappointed eyes peered over the mask covering his nose and mouth. Sad not because he was wearing a hospital mask protecting him from germs due to his fragile immune system. No, his eyes were downcast because I was not Father Joe.

Being a visiting priest can bring such sadness to little eyes. I've come to expect and understand it. Little eyes of children who are wondering where their "Father Joe" is, and who is this trying to take his place?

A visiting priest can also bring delight. I love to remind people as a visiting priest they go to confession to me and I literally carry their sins out of town! That's one way of "shaking the dust from your feet!" Matthew 10:14

But on this particular day, I truly wished I was Father Joe, so I could give familiar comfort to this little child who had been recently diagnosed with a very serious disease. I did the second best thing I could: I gave him a blessing from the Church, invoking healing, and kept him in prayer all day, even as I wrote these thoughts.

As Christians we are to be joy filled persons. Pope Francis reminds us in Evangelii Gaudium (The Joy of the Gospel) we shouldn't look like we are coming from a funeral when we proclaim the Gospel. At Christmastime, the Church's liturgy is filled with refrains such as, "Joy to the World, the Lord has come," or "Peace on earth!"

But sometimes we don't feel so joyful. Sometimes we feel as if we are coming from a funeral. Many funerals.

The sacristy is a place where the priest vests and vessels are prepared for the Holy Sacrifice of the Mass. It is designed to be a place of preparation. A place of prayer for the priest and ministers getting ready for Mass.

But normally it is a center of chaos. Kind of like the kitchen before Thanksgiving dinner. There mom is, preparing for a huge dinner, and what are all the guests doing? They are standing in the kitchen talking and gawking!

I was preparing for Mass when Betty came in the sacristy. She had some things to review with me. Occasionally God thumps me over the head and says

"Listen!" So I listened. We talked about her family, about her prayer life, and finally I answered her question about who would water the flowers while she would be gone for the next couple of weeks.

It was the last time I would have the opportunity to speak with her. Tragically she slipped and fell the day before Christmas, causing irreparable damage.

It was both Betty and the little disappointed eyes I was reflecting upon during a beautiful song at Mass whose lyrics went something like, "The baby Jesus brought peace and healing to the world. An end of strife and sorrow."

"Where did Jesus do this? I don't think Betty's family or the little boy would see it that way." I thought to myself, and then immediately felt guilty for thinking and feeling this way.

I'm a priest, in the middle of Mass, presiding at the Holy Sacrifice of the Mass, how could I think such thoughts? I knew they were not sinful thoughts, but thoughts I would have to explore further with the Lord.

The words of the festive song filled my ears but the pall of sadness covered my heart on the drive home. Violating my own personal rule, I checked my e-mails before going to the chapel to pray mid-day prayer. It was on Outlook e-mail God gave me His answer.

It was a Christmas greeting e-mail from a young man whose father I walked with in his final stages of cancer over twenty years ago. The young man now married with children and a law enforcement officer just wanted to let me know what was going on in his life.

I remember well his eyes as a child while I was ministering to his family in their time of sadness and bewilderment. He concluded his Christmas e-mail with, "Take care and may God bless you and may He grant blessings to you and others through the ministry of your priesthood. Be assured that you are in my prayers." He, who was at one time confused why God was allowing such tragic events, had become a man of faith and hope.

Ahh, that's the answer. Hope. The song I heard was beautiful, but incomplete. What Jesus brought us was not an easy path, but a path filled with hope; for He is present with us every step of the way. Hope the cross is not the end, but only a beginning.

The little boy had reason to be disappointed in me. I was not "his" father, his shepherd, his parish priest. But I am certain when he finally sees Father Joe, his eyes will be filled with hope, just as I brought the hope of Christ's resurrection to another young boy twenty years ago. A hope only Christ can bring through the Sacraments and the priesthood.

Hope is truly joyous to the world!

14 A QUICKER GATE TO HEAVEN?

"When the young man left home, accompanied by the angel, the dog followed Tobiah out and went along with them. Both journeyed along, and when the first night came, they camped beside the Tigris River." Tobit 6:2

In the seminary I was taught everything, and I mean everything is fodder for homilies. With that in mind, I am often reflecting how different experiences, trivia, current television shows, or newspaper articles can be used in a homily. This is something Jesus also did.

Jesus was raised by a carpenter. He understood wood and probably was also skilled in blacksmithing.

As a teenager, into his twenty's, Jesus labored in Nazareth as a carpenter. The original Greek word for a carpenter, according to James Martin, S.J., was "tekton." Martin writes most contemporary scholars say it's likely Jesus and Joseph were general craftsmen who would have made doors, tables, lamp stands and plows. They also might have built stone walls and assisted with the construction of houses.

This being said, Jesus was not a fisherman, a farmer, nor a shepherd. But so many of his parables were about things other than carpentry, and in fact I can think of no parable or analogy in which he used carpentry as an example. Couldn't you hear him saying, "To what can I compare the kingdom of heaven? It is like sawing a piece of lumber. Measure twice, and cut once."

Okay, not the best example. Or perhaps he would have joked to his apostles, "Do you know what kind of saw it takes to cut the Sea of Galilee in half? A see-saw!" Well, you get the point. Jesus used the same skills of observation I was taught relating the Gospel to everyday events and happenings of his day. Even if these were events he did not participate.

Airports are a fascinating place for observing and relating what you observe to the gospel message. Arriving at an airport, I give myself a pep talk using such phrases such as: "Calm. It's okay. You are safe. Whatever goes wrong is okay. Whatever goes right is a blessing." You have heard of computers having "safe modes?" I call my airport mode, the "slow mode." Nothing is going to bother me.

"You want me to take off my shoes? Sure, no problem. My coat? Sure. You want me to strip naked? Sure, no problem." I have found the best way to be assured you are separated from the herd of people and frisked, is to wear a clerical collar. Sometimes I feel like a TSA magnet.

The whole experience at the airport is a parallel to me of life's journey. You enter the airport terminal excited about going somewhere. You then wait in line. And wait. And wait. Then you find out you are in the wrong line. Perhaps even in the wrong terminal. (I

wonder why they call it an airport "terminal?" It's not the conclusion. Perhaps we should call it the airport commencement when you take off, and then you land at the airport terminal.)

The excitement, the wait, the thinking you are going to get somewhere, and then a change and more waiting reminds me of the pregnancy process for a baby. "Time to go! Oops, false start... wait....here we go!"

At the airport, finally after all the waiting, then the cattle chute narrows and you are strip searched, patted down, and photo rayed where they can scope every body part, finding your way to the light of the other side. Birth!

After collecting your belongings of coats, baggage, wallet, keys, kids, we then wait again at another gate. Lots of gates. Another analogy of the many choices we have in life. Throughout life we are collecting: honor, jobs, forming a family, possessions. Like life, we eventually have to let these possessions go and place them in the overhead bin, only to find we have too much stuff! Carefully we pass our overstuffed carry-on to the stewardess hoping to see it again at the end of the trip.

This process of handing things over reminds me of the funeral vigil rite words, *"All the ties that knit us together in this lifetime, does not unravel in death."* Our loved ones and passions on earth, like our baggage, we hope to see once again at the end of the journey, but in order to do so, we must "let go of our baggage."

Sitting in the gate waiting for the arrival of my plane is filled with observation, especially for a celibate priest (meaning I don't have any children to keep track of so I can keep track of what everyone else is doing). Sometimes, if I am on Church business, I travel in my clerics. If I am on personal time, I don't. There are advantages to both.

With clerics I get the TSA pat down, and the inevitable opportunity to evangelize, sometimes by a conversation, but most often by glances. It's fun to watch people try to crane their necks to see what the priest is reading in the gate lounge. Curious lot of people. They try to be so causal about it. Sometimes they are bolder and will turn to you and say, "I guess we should be safe with you traveling with us!" Talk about a heavy responsibility! Thankfully the 1970's airport movies are not as popular with Sammy Davis Junior portraying a priest! Then they really expect you to entertain as well as prayerfully protect!

Without clerics I am more dressed like Jesus. He did not wear the robes of a Pharisee or priest of his time. No, he dressed like a carpenter's son. Ordinary. Yet, even dressed ordinary, we can attract attention. Being in my "slow mode" dressed in blue jeans and a shirt, I will often attract attention because I am not flustered.

And then there are the little ladies, who have a "priest radar," seeing right through my disguise, and will sit right next to me striking up a conversation. That and the fallen away Catholic always finds me in blue jeans. If I was dressed as a priest, they would avoid me. But sitting next to me, the conversation begins innocently, but then naturally goes to, "So.... What do you do for a living?" It's amazing how the Holy Spirit dresses me as I am needed.

At the gate, there are various different emotions throughout the space. As I would look around, I always see military. So young, fresh, and eager. Sometimes they are exhausted, or simply looking like middle school children playing video games on their phones dressed up like GI Joes. Generally there is always the person who is obviously struggling with cancer or some life threatening disease, either coming or going to a treatment center. Or coming or going to a relative's home, perhaps for the last time.

Then there are the families. Often excited. Perhaps going to one of the Disney parks or the grandparents' home. The parents sometimes sharing their excitement, but more often than not, engrossed in their own cell phones knowing the kids are safe in this in-between space of travel.

Of course one cannot forget the airline and airport employees. The haggard folk at the counter trying to do whatever work is necessary to get the flight ready, constantly being interrupted by passengers checking their tickets or trying to find the right gate.

The employees I enjoy the most are the airport custodians. They move slowly and deliberately through the crowds, intent only on one thing, and one thing only: to be of service and pick up trash and clean up after people. Rarely are they interrupted. I wonder why? Do we passengers assume they are unintelligent? Often these humble servants know the way through the airport maze much better than anyone else. They sometimes look sad, but more often than not, they are laughing and joking with one another. Frequently in different languages. They are so intelligent; they are bi- and tri-lingual.

As one looks down the crowded hallways filled with people, one cannot forget there is a pecking order in the airline business. Smartly dressed, young, vibrant and at least three to four abreast with seemingly brand new luggage rolling behind them, here comes the airplane crew! The masses of passengers part as they approach the gate, and they get out their magic cards to enter the forbidden zone first. Rarely conversing with passengers, but laughing and conversing with one another, they are soon gone down the gateway, never to be fully sighted again except for perhaps the back of their head and the muffled voice though the intercom.

The gate itself is a wonderful metaphor of life. Many different people, different ways, different roles and purposes but all waiting and preparing to go on a short journey to reach a final destination. The gate, to me, is life here on earth. Some at the gate have carefully prepared for the journey and know exactly where they are going; some have little or no care in the world. They just know they are going somewhere else.

Once the plane arrives, the most peculiar thing happens. Two chutes, both lined with colored theatre ropes, are placed between the passengers and the waiting plane. These chutes with the colorful ropes both lead to the same plane, but one chute has a red carpeted foot mat. A mat normally used to wipe one's feet, but this particular mat has words such as "Priority Passengers" or "Gold Elite Passengers. "

In order for one to walk through this matted and notably designated chute, one must pay more money. This allows one to enter the plane first in order for them to be served a warm wash towel for their hands. An observer might wonder if this herd of passengers is dirty, requiring them to clean their feet before they enter the cabin and their hands once they arrive. Then, as the non-priority and non-gold elite passengers pass by, the elite passengers are drinking beverages of their choice with their clean hands and feet.

The separation between these two herds continues in flight. Once the plane is airborne, an announcement is made directing the non-priority passengers to not use the front restroom which is reserved only for the passengers who were cleaned before take-off. After which to accent this point, a see through curtain is drawn in order to prevent any such movement between these two groups of people.

Finally, at the end of the flight again, the priority passengers are washed down before landing. As priority passengers they of course arrive first on the tarmac of the anticipated airport. Kind of reminds me of when we, as children, would try to outreach one another in the station wagon when we crossed a state line. "I got there first!" we would exclaim in delight!

Metaphor of life? *They came to Capernaum and, once inside the house, he began to ask them, "What were you arguing about on the way?" But they remained silent. They had been discussing among themselves on the way who was the greatest." (Mark 9:33-34)*

I don't blame passengers. More leg room and a warm towel is definitely the way to get to your destination. I do blame the airlines for taking advantage of our human vulnerabilities of wanting to believe we are more special than another. In God's eyes we are all equally His children. In the eyes of the world, we often are not.

"Whoever causes one of these little ones who believe in me to sin, it would be better for him to have a great millstone hung around his neck and to be drowned in the depths of the sea." Matthew 18:6.

Sometimes it's rather silly for us to create such separations with see-through curtains and "special" red carpeted foot mat chutes. We are all going to the same place, that is, eternity. The question is, will we accept His loving embrace or will we refuse it. How we lived upon this earth; how we waited and traveled; serving and loving His other children is what counts.

"Then the King will say to those on his right, 'Come, you who are blessed by my Father, inherit the kingdom prepared for you from the foundation of the world." Matthew 25:34.

These are the ones who will have the special red carpet entrance.

Scripture obviously doesn't say much about airports or air travel, although there are some who see air travel in Isaiah 60:8, *"Who are these that fly like a cloud, and like doves to their windows?"* Personally I think this might be pushing it a little bit. Isaiah was speaking about the Israelites returning home from the Babylonian exile, not airplanes.

But the Scripture does have much to say about metaphors and the importance of keeping our eyes open to the Kingdom of God on earth. *"Do you not yet understand or comprehend? Are your hearts hardened? Do you have eyes and not see, ears and not hear?"* Mark 8: 17-18.

They were right in the seminary. Everything is fodder for homilies. Even airports and air travel.

"Then I saw another angel flying in midair, and he had the eternal gospel to proclaim to those who live on the earth--to every nation, tribe, language and people." Revelations 14:6.

15 PILLARS OF THE EARTH

"He raises the needy from the dust; from the ash heap lifts up the poor, To seat them with nobles and make a glorious throne their heritage. "For the pillars of the earth are the Lord's, and he has set the world upon them." First Book of Samuel 2:8

I must be a "pillar magnet" a brother priest told me recently. In our newly renovated Cathedral, we have space now for the priests to be seated and participate in the Mass in the sanctuary. The fullness of the Catholic Church can be seen and experienced when the priests are gathered around their bishop in the celebration of the Eucharist at the Cathedral of our Diocese.

This was the scene recently in our diocese when a priest from another diocese was ordained our bishop and welcomed by the priests and laity alike. What a glorious ceremony, filled with richness, tradition, and joy.

"So, how did you like the ordination?" I was asked.

"Well...." I responded. "Here we go!" He said.

I, like most men (I hope), struggle with the expression of emotions. Sometimes I don't experience emotions others obviously have. Other times, I do experience emotions, but most certainly don't want to discuss them, dissect them, or expose them. Sometimes a commercial will get me teary eyed. Remember the Pizza Hut commercial of the little boy in the outfield, praying they would not hit the ball to him? I can relate to that boy, and tears can come to my eyes.

With such bizarre gamete of emotions, from no emotions to emotions over a commercial, the last thing I want to do is discuss them! I really don't like emotions. They get in the way!

Continuing my conversation, "Yes, I enjoyed the ordination, but I didn't see a thing! I was stuck behind a pillar! No matter where I line up before Mass at the Cathedral, no matter what, I seem to get seated behind the same pillar!" It was then I was called a "pillar magnet."

I do have feelings, emotions. Although I relate better to what St. Ignatius of the 16th century called them: "movements of the heart." That sounds manlier doesn't it? Movements of the heart.

The hearts of the priests throughout a bishop's ordination is not only moving, they are quaking! So many emotions. When a president is elected and takes office by inauguration, we know quite a bit about them. Generally after 3 ½ years of campaigning, we know too much about the person. But a newly appointed bishop is not known by his new flock.

Anxiety, joy, nervousness, and delight are all moving about. While we men try to hide it, we are a mess. "Will I make a good first impression?" "Will I be moved immediately?" "What will change?" Very similar to a parish accepting a new pastor, but magnified.

Of all the promises and vows a priest makes, the promise of obedience to the bishop and his successors is the most important and challenging. When a young man places his hands into a bishop's hands at ordination, he generally knows the bishop in front of him. But he doesn't see into the future. He does not see who this bishop's successors will be.

A bishop determines where a priest lays his head down to sleep each night, what sheep he will love (or smell like as Pope Francis would say), and what part of the Body of Christ he will serve. A bishop is the voice of Jesus, the Good Shepherd. A good priest wants this voice in his life, but those darn "movements of the heart" make him feel emotions he would rather ignore.

"You seem to be a pillar magnet!" I was told. Reflecting on those pillars of that Cathedral during the ordination, for it was truly the only thing I could see, I remembered another time in that same church. I was a boy, asleep on my father's lap, probably 4 or 5. I remember the security I felt there amongst those pillars.

Or I remember playing games with the little mouse living under the pews, seeing him poke his head in and out of the little mouse hole carved out of the pews footings. (No there really wasn't a mouse, but the pews had little oval holes in their base that looked like mouse homes)

Or the time Bishop Mark K. Carroll pointing up into the cupola and boomed, "The Holy Family is looking down upon you." , and I looking up seeing the many windows, I, as a 5 year old boy, understood the Holy Family must have an apartment behind one of those windows. (I really have a vivid imagination! I even saw the shadow of Mary passing by!)

Pillars. The strength of our faith. "The earth and all its inhabitants will quake, but I have firmly set its pillars." Psalm 75:4. Our faith and lives are built upon the pillars of our faith. A bishop is the visible expression of those pillars. The Book of the Gospels place over the head of the newly ordained bishop as a canopy shows that he, the bishop, now is part of the pillars of the church, a rock, upon which the church has been built (Mt. 16:18).

Amid the varied movements of the priest hearts, is the assent of faith. Yes, Lord, I do believe! Yes, it is so! Just as a little boy feeling secure in the lap of his earthly father among the pillars of the Cathedral, so now that boy, a priest among the People of God, feels secure with a new shepherd who will teach, sanctify, and govern his new flock.

Perhaps we all have become "pillar magnets," for we all need a pillar under which to live our faith.

16 PRIESTS ARE MEN TOO!

"This is why I speak to them in parables, because 'they look but do not see and hear but do not listen or understand.' Matthew 3:13

She looked at us like we had two heads! Or maybe none!

When priests go out to dinner, we often get gawks. Sometimes because we are in our Roman collars. Sometimes because people recognize us and realize priests really do eat too! But sometimes for other reasons.

We do however try to disguise ourselves. But being men, we do a poor job of it. Most of us have two wardrobes: black slacks and blue jeans. It's funny to be in an airport. I usually can spot a priest a mile away, especially if he is not wearing clerics. Most of us don what is commonly referred to as the "priest on vacation" look.

It's not a look of holiness. Or a look of relief of being away from the responsibilities of the parish. No, it's more practical than that. Having basically two pants, the "priest on vacation" fashion is black pants and a button down shirt of color. I can't quite put my finger on what makes the look so recognizable. Maybe it's because we look and probably act out of place. Trying to fit in too hard. Like a teenager trying to be inconspicuous, only to stick out like a sore thumb. We don't always do a good job fitting in.

A priest friend of mine and I decided to treat ourselves to a dinner out on the town. We went to our favorite restaurant, only to find a forty-five minute wait for a table. Odd, we thought. Maybe they were running a special we didn't know about.

Off to another restaurant, only to find a longer wait time. Finally we choose a smaller diner. It too was crowded, but we managed to find a booth in the back and slipped in for a comfortable dinner.

The teenaged waitress came to our table to take our drink order. After we gave her our order, we asked, "Why are all the restaurants so crowded?" It was then she gave us the gawk only a teenager can give, which says, "What planet are you from!?!"

Shaking her head as if we were too dumb to warrant an answer, she left to get us menus. "Oh well," I thought, "must be a festival or something." Since I do not read the newspaper, I am sometimes out of the loop.

Being a priest, I can sometimes be rather oblivious to the obvious. Such as the time when I went to a small Italian restaurant in my clerics with two other priests, also in clerics. We were enjoying a nice meal,

 but the restaurant was rather small, so when a very large group of people came in, it suddenly became very crowded.

Pulling a number of tables together, this party pretty much took over the restaurant, leaving us priests separated, but surrounded by this new assembly of patrons.

I didn't notice at first, but then I kept feeling stolen glances towards our table and could hear slight murmuring. Not thinking much of it, I ignored it, but then it seemed to get quiet. Too quiet. Looking up, I wondered if the large group was perhaps praying before their meal.

No. Not praying. Definitely not praying. Not sure what they were doing, but definitely not praying.

Looking past one of the men seated at a table near us I noticed a large white index card reserving the table for the group. The card said in bold letters: "RESERVED for the Mid-City Atheist Group.

Well that explains it. I wonder if they thought we were new recruits!

Our teenaged waiter finally returns with our menus and asked, "So did you figure out why it's so crowded tonight?"

"Not really," I replied, "some festival?"

"Yeah, you could say that," she said handing us red menus shaped in a heart, "we have some great specials on our items that can be shared by two." Pointing to the tables' centerpiece which was red and pink flowers set in a vase filled with little candy hearts with sweet sayings on them, with a mocking face she said, "It's Valentine's day!"

I suddenly realized she wasn't gawking at us funny because we were priests, but because we were men oblivious to the obvious! Yes, priests are men too!

17 RESPONSES AND CRICKETS

[Solomon's Wedding Procession] "Who is this coming up from the desert, like columns of smoke Perfumed with myrrh and frankincense, with all kinds of exotic powders?" Song of Songs 3:6

All I heard were crickets. No, really. Crickets. I was in a country parish and had just proclaimed the opening greeting, "The Lord be with you." And all I heard were crickets. Anything out of the ordinary will throw off the usual response.

"And he ran to Eli and said, "Here I am; you called me." But Eli said, "I did not call; go back and lie down." So he went and lay down." (1 Samuel 3:5)

"Lord, if it's you," Peter replied, "tell me to come to you on the water." (Matthew 14:8) Or "He fled naked, leaving his garment behind," (Mark 14:52)

It would be understandable if the Lord called to us audibly when we were asleep, or if we saw Jesus walking on the water, or if we witnessed Jesus being arrested in the Garden of Gethsemane, but my greeting was the same welcome the people hear every time they go to Mass. Still, crickets.

What was so unusual about this Mass? It was a wedding Mass. Why should that make a difference you might think? Oh, because at a wedding Mass, everything is out of the ordinary.

The Church's Nuptial Mass, in the book, is exactly like a Sunday Mass (with no collection) except for after the homily. After the homily the couple answers questions about their freedom to marry, exchange vows, exchange rings if it is a custom, and that's it! Nothing more. Really!

No questioning the congregation if the couple should marry. That only happens in Days of our Lives soap opera. No crashing waves of the sea behind the couple. That only happens on the Bachelorette. And most certainly no rice throwing. That is a custom of the ancient Assyrians, Hebrews, and Egyptians, symbolizing fruitfulness, fertility, and good wishes.

Even though the Church's ritual is simple, weddings can become complicated. For instance the procession. Macy's parade is less complicated than some wedding processions I've seen.

There was the "Monty Hall" procession. Monty Hall was the game show host who would have contestants guess what was behind numerous doors. In one particular church I served, the architect wanted to show from the Eucharistic celebration we are sent to all four corners of the earth to proclaim what we have received. So the church was designed with many doors, all leading to the four directions.

The bride and groom thought it would be a great idea for the groomsmen to enter two different doors, and the bridesmaids to arrive at the other two doors, all meeting (theoretically) in the middle aisle. I, having some understanding of the chaos which would ensue, vetoed the grand idea at the rehearsal. However the bride and groom used the ole "Once Father's at the altar, he can't do anything" wedding trick.

So I walked down the aisle with my altar servers in tow, I turn to see the doors begin to open and close with arms and hands waving, frantically trying to give directions. There they came down the aisle, from all four corners the earth. However the earth moved and they didn't quite get the pairing correct, and suddenly groomsmen were reaching out to groomsmen, and bridesmaids to other maids.

It all worked out in the end, as they all huddled in the middle aisle, and forth from the huddle came the couples, two by two, male and female, just like Noah's ark. I was old and wise enough pastor by this time to simply chuckle at the chaos. They were right, there was nothing I could do, none the less, the homily was about the importance of obedience to each other and the church, and a bit longer than usual since the bride and groom had to kneel through the homily.

And then there was the "Bravehart Wedding Procession." William Wallace and even King Edward I of England would have been impressed by the band of groomsmen processing down the church aisle behind bagpipes, proudly wearing their knee high pleated kilts. I choose not to question how authentic the wearing of the kilts was. I thought it best to presume they used prudent and modest judgment, knowing full well this was not the case.

Of course I can't forget the many processions with the adorable ring bearers, carrying multi thousand dollar rings, only to fling the pillow, projecting the snowy white cushion in one direction, while the sparkling diamond ring shoots like a falling star in the other direction. The sound of a silver diamond ring on a terrazzo or porcelain floor makes a magical sound, only  interrupted by the gasp and stifled cry of the bride.

Perhaps I am wrong. Sometimes things out of the ordinary do receive the usual response. Now, if I could only get Catholics to respond like normal at a wedding.

18 THE GYM

"Do you not know that the runners in the stadium all run in the race, but only one wins the prize? Run so as to win. Every athlete exercises discipline in every way. They do it to win a perishable crown, but we an imperishable one. Thus I do not run aimlessly; I do not fight as if I were shadowboxing. No, I drive my body and train it, for fear that, after having preached to others, I myself should be disqualified." 1 Corinthians 9: 24-27

Like I was. Like the many young priests I have written about, the young man seated before me was self-assured, energetic, and strong in his beliefs.

Unfortunately, my response to his confidence, energy, and conviction was not immediately accepted.

My response to a series of suggestions was the same response of, "That ain't goin to happen."I could tell he was somewhat frustrated with me but being the young professional he was, he tried mightily to hide it. I felt sorry for him....kind of.

When people come to the retreat center I have the privilege of being a part of, I often ask what they think is the most important thing to do first. It is a trick question, and rarely do they answer correctly. Since the question is being addressed by a Catholic priest to a person who is beginning a retreat, their natural answer is "To pray." Or perhaps even deeper, but just as wrong, "To listen to the Lord."

No the first thing one must do on a retreat is to take care of one's body. For this reason our retreat center has many bedrooms with comfortable beds. Down the hall from the chapel is the dining room where delicious meals are prepared. These meals, of course, have been specially blessed, so no bad cholesterol or other bad things are found in it. This way a person can eat till their full and not worry about it.

Then, and only after taking proper care of ones body can a person begin to either talk to the Lord and/or listen to the Lord. I remind people if they come on a retreat and only get rest and proper food, then the retreat is successful. Often times it will be the drive home after rest and food, that will they begin a conversation with the Lord or have the Lord speak to them.

Our bodies are a key component to our spirituality. It more than "houses" the spirit. As Saint John Paul II taught, there is a "theology of the body," creating a vital connection with our spiritual souls. If we are too tired or hungry, our souls are affected. Generally the enemy tempts us through our body. The devil uses our body to get to our spiritual souls.

Therefore with all of this in mind, I kind of felt sorry for the young man whom I was not cooperating with...kind of. Throughout my priesthood I have understood the importance of this body and spiritual soul connection; therefore I have always tried to exercise. But let me be honest. My exercise regimen is consistently inconsistent. To help me, I have joined various gyms. Thus the conversation I was having with this young man who was helping me to switch gym memberships.

First he took down lots of information. I felt like I was filling out paperwork at the doctor's office. This went pretty well, although he didn't understand why I put down my staff and bishop as points of contact. I tried to explain I didn't have a spouse, children, or roommate, therefore if I keeled over in a "spinning class" which I thought would be filled with little old ladies "spinning yarn" only to find muscular slender ladies who cycled circles around me on stationary bicycles all the while talking about their spouses, children, careers, and mother in laws, effortlessly without seemingly to break a sweat or need a break; if I did keel over there, the closest persons to come and discreetly get my broken and fatigued body out of there would be my staff.

Then he took me on a tour of the gym which began the series of "That ain't goin' to happen!" For one exercise room, I was instructed I would need "toe socks." Not knowing what this new fashion is and owning only 1970's white tube socks, I suggested "That ain't goin to happen." Then he showed a room full of very large balls. Balls not for hitting, or kicking, but for doing sit ups on or lifting weights. Again, "That ain't goin to happen." Finally he valiantly tried to sign me up for something called a "boot camp." With only the understanding of military boot camps, and remembering my one, count it, ONE spinning class, I gave a big, "That ain't goin to happen."

He was finally catching on I simply wanted to run on a treadmill and lift some weights, when he pulled out the tanning brochures and said, "And I suppose tanning ain't goin to happen either?"

Yes, I felt sorry for him...kind of. He was offering me a chance to change my body. An opportunity to help my spiritual soul. Exercise of our bodies is very important for our spiritual souls, although I suspect if I joined the boot camp, my spiritual soul would see the Lord much sooner than He was expecting me.

THE GYM PART II:
PHYSICAL AND SPIRITUAL TRAINERS

"The glory of young men is their strength, but the splendor of old men is their gray hair." Proverbs 20:29

It was an unlikely pair. The young man was muscular, light on his feet, and barely breathing. The older woman obviously past mid-life, was taking two steps to the young man's one, and excitably chatting. Round and round they went. Finally, they exited the rubber track and went to a machine.

Judiciously the woman sat on the padded bench, placed her feet in the contraption, and slowly moved the weighted lever back and forth. All the while the young man smiling and encouraging her by counting the reps and giving firm words of reinforcement.

At times it looked like the older woman wanted to abandon the exercise, or would get so animated about what she was telling the young man, she would get distracted. Softly and with determination, the young trainer would keep her on track, consistently easing her through the repetitions and various exercise machines.

You can learn a lot about spirituality at the gym. This is not new. For over 3000 years a gym was used for both physical and intellectual education. I was taught in the seminary, everything and all experiences a priest has, is fodder for homilies. I find this is true. Similar to the conversion of stewardship when you see everything as a gift from the Lord, once you put on priest "glasses," nothing looks the same again.

So when I saw the young man and older woman exercising in the gym, I was struck by the parallel to our spiritual life. The gym offers what they call

"personal training." Here is what one gym advertises:

"Our personal trainers are all certified, highly-trained fitness experts. Our personal training programs are designed to empower you and help you meet your goals. Our goal is to motivate, educate and ultimately to help you look and feel better...."

Sounds pretty good huh? Looking around the gym, I notice a lot of people working out with others, often with a personal trainer. But I realize something odd. The personal trainers are all young and athletic! I also notice the trainee is more often, how shall I say, less young and athletic!

As I climb onto a machine with a sign reading, "This machine is excellent for isolating the quadriceps muscles in which many people like to use for pre-exhausting their quadriceps before moving to leg presses," I began to think about trainers. I also began to think why in the world someone would desire to "pre-exhaust" their quadriceps! Sometimes just getting to the gym, I feel "pre-exhausted."

In the Christian life we also have "trainers." I was introduced to this relationship for the first time in the seminary.

He was the physical opposite of a health club trainer: older, not in the prime of his physical condition with little to no athletic prowess. But in contrast, his spiritual body bulked with wisdom, experience, and patience. Highly certified by experience in walking in the spiritual world, he was what one would call an expert, but in the spiritual world, an expert is often called a guru or a sage. These would be the very last things he would call himself, for a true "expert" in spirituality, one must become weak and insignificant.

Thomas Merton wrote: "The whole purpose of spiritual direction is to penetrate beneath the surface of a man's life, to get behind the façade of conventional gestures and attitudes which he presents to the world, and to bring out his inner spiritual freedom, his inmost truth, which is what we call the likeness of Christ in his soul." (Spiritual Direction and Meditation, p.16)

I remember clearly going to this spiritual trainer in the seminary with a very deep and flawless awareness into my budding vocation. Realizing I began the seminary training to become a priest too hastily, I expressed my insight, and I nervously blurted out, "I think God is not calling me to be a priest, but rather first, to be a better Christian man. Once I establish virtue as a Christian man, then I can begin again in the seminary training to be a priest."

My spiritual trainer leaned back in his rocker, paused, and closed his eyes. Expecting praise and affirmation, I leaned forward, receptive to his words. Opening his eyes, his expression was gentle, filled with kindness, and compassion, and he said: "I think that is a bunch of horse manure!"

Suddenly my façade fell. Confused how my spiritual director could look so gentle while tearing my carefully laid arguments to quit down. Like a health club trainer, confident, affirming, but determined in the midst of my chatter, my spiritual director kept me on task.

Today I am so thankful for his confidence in me which allowed me to continue and finally be ordained. Now after close to 24 years of being in the "gym," I have the honor of being a "trainer" for others. I suspect you too have spiritual trainers in your life. A parent, spouse, priest, or grandparent.

Yes, you can learn a lot about spirituality in a gym. Now if only I can figure out this "pre-exhaustion" thing! Perhaps they are talking about purgatory!

19 OUR LORD DIDN'T MAKE NO UGLY CROSSES

"The message of the cross is foolishness to those who are perishing, but to us who are being saved it is the power of God." 1 Corinthians 1:18

Art causes emotions. Emotions generally are good emotions or distasteful emotions. Yes, there is a large range of emotions, and emotions are just feelings, neither morally good nor evil, but generally all emotions are welcomed or unwelcomed; good or distasteful.

On vacations, I enjoy praying before Mass like a "regular" parishioner in the churches I visit. As I sat in one particular church, I was experiencing distasteful emotions. Looking at the crucifix hanging over the altar, the distasteful emotion wasn't of the theological type, which is, moved by the suffering seen on the cross, or the manner in which the artist depicted the horrific scene. No, the crucifix was just ugly, that's all. Ugly....at least to me.

The wood used for the cross and corpus looked like butter. All I could see when I looked at the cross was the butter sculptures at the state fair depicting either cows, or farmers, or some other rural scene. Somehow seeing Jesus as a butter sculpture wasn't right. It was ugly.

Walking to the other side of the church to pray my rosary, I saw the full of the ugliness of the crucifix. Not only was it buttery, I saw the corpus was one with the cross. The artist did not even separate the buttery corpus from the buttery cross beams. It made the crucifix appear to have been a poured cast. Like a plastic toy.

By now, the ugliness was a distraction. Even though I did not like the crucifix, I kept looking at it. I guess I like butter. Creamy butter. But surly this was not the draw to it. No, the more I looked, the less I prayed. I think they call this a "distraction" in prayer. I began to think what I would do to make the crucifix better. Different color. Different posture of the corpus. Separating the corpus from the cross.

Shaking myself away from my thoughts, I concentrated on the words of the Hail Mary I should be praying. When praying the rosary I try to enter into the prayer by feeling what the persons in each mystery might have felt. What would Mary have felt at the foot of the cross? Anger? Bewilderment? Would she have seen this as ugly?

Appalling yes, but ugly? Perhaps the scene was ugly, but never the person of Jesus. For even in a ghastly death grey, she would have seen beauty in our Lord's face. A beauty a mother can see and a beauty perhaps the Angel Gabriel prepared her to experience.

Returning my gaze on the crucifix, I began to look at it differently. The buttery tone was smooth and even, taking on the light rays of the stained glass windows. Slowly reflecting the hues and tints of the sun setting through the windows. A darker stained wood would never have mirrored such colors.

Then I began to see the corpus connected to the wood beams of the cross. Perhaps this was not a mistake. Perhaps the artist intended for the two to be of one material. It was as if Jesus became one with the cross. No more did He struggle with "Father let this cup pass," or "My God, my God why have you abandoned me?" He was at peace and one with the cross. His cross. My cross.

Slowly finishing the rosary, I began to look around at the people coming into the church for Mass. Genuflecting to the tabernacle with the buttery cross whose corpus and wood beam were one. As I began to look into their faces, I could see art there too, invoking feelings.

I began to look at them, reflecting upon the many faces of parishioners I've served in the past. Some faces invoked feelings of warmth and love, others of challenges and uneasiness. As a priest, like Jesus, I had my faithful disciples and disgruntled Pharisees, my friends and my adversaries, which is sad because we all love the same Lord. It was parishioners I struggled to accept as they were, and the parishioners who struggled to accept me which invoked feelings I would rather ignore.

Gazing upon the once ugly cross again, I realized I need to look at my challenges and certain people through different lenses, through the eyes of Mary. Then I can see the beautiful art our Lord has drawn in so many people, all being one with their individual weighty crosses. Crosses He carried so well that He became one with. Just as He is one with His People, even me.

20 WALKING OR PRIESTLY MEDITATING???

"They were on the way, going up to Jerusalem, and Jesus went ahead of them." Mark 10:32

Every Lent I struggle with what to give up for Lent. I instruct others to do things or give up things for Lent, but what about me? Should I pray more? Eat less? Sure, but our Lenten observances should have a lasting effect, not just for the 40 days of Lent.

"Oh Father, but you are so busy!" I often hear this, but priests are no busier than anyone else. In fact, I would say less hectic! Without the responsibilities of a spouse, children, home ownership, or worry of the next meal, our lives do not have many of the busyness of a husband or father of children. We are busy, but our busyness should be of the Lord, and often I find myself busy about things not of the Lord.

If you want to get people's attention, walk around the neighborhood in clerics. People in the Midwest when the weather is good, are walkers! They walk their neighborhoods, parks, or just around the block. I think walking has taken the place of sitting on the front porch. But a priest walking around the neighborhood in his black clerics will definitely get attention!

One warm summer's evening I went for a walk wearing my clerics. When I was newly ordained I noticed some priests would wear white clerics. Presuming these priests were "liberal," since they choose not to wear the "traditional" black clerics, I later understood. In Kansas and in the South American missions where these priests served, the hot sun makes wearing black clerics unbearable in the heat. So if you are going to be outside for any length of time, black clerics are not advisable!

This particular summer evening was warm, but the sun was not beating down making me uncomfortable. As I grow older wearing of clerics becomes less apparent to me. I often forget whether I am in "uniform" or not. Walking I notice a woman looking at me unusually, I wondered what was up. Perhaps she had a question for me.

Pope Francis says we should take the Gospel to the street. I found when I walk around a neighborhood, especially if I am walking a dog, I get many gawks and questions. People feel comfortable talking with a priest when he is out and about. This woman was no different.

Walking towards me, she stopped. I could tell she wanted to say something but was hesitating so I cordially greeted her. She returned the greeting, and asked, "I was unsure whether to stop you. Are you just walking, or priestly meditating?" I chuckled, and replied I was "just walking." Spending a couple of minutes in conversation about the weather and the happenings at the parish, we went our separate ways.

Her question however remained on my mind. "What a silly question!" I thought, "Why do people think we priests can't do normal things like walking without making it into some clerical, churchy thing? We are just normal folk really."

"What are you going to give up for Lent, Father?" the fifth grade girl asked. I proceeded to tell her how during Lent we should develop practices of bringing the Lord into the normal things we do in life, such as when we fast, we should do it for the Lord, or else it's just dieting. When we give money to the Church and to the poor, we should be doing it for the Lord, not because we get something in return such as thanksgiving or Catholic school education. When we pray, it should be because we love God, not because we have to pray.

Reflecting on my answer to the little girl on my walk back to the rectory from the parish school, I felt pretty good about my response. I even said a prayer in thanksgiving to the Lord for giving me the right words. I knew I was correct. All the practices we do in the church, in fact, everything we do have to be done for the Lord, or else it is self-serving.

Suddenly I stopped and laughed. The children on the playground probably thought I was a little cracked. I realized I was no longer "just walking" home; I was "priestly meditating!" I was in fact practicing what I just preached: not just walking, but doing it with and for the Lord.

She had it right, the lady who wondered if I was meditating rather than walking. I figured out what I was going to do for Lent. This Lent I am going to keep my normal busy, but make a conscious effort to direct my busyness to the Lord. Not just walking, but priestly meditating!

"Unless the LORD builds the house, the builders labor in vain." Psalm 127:1

21 WHAT A PRIEST LEAVES BEHIND

"Jesus then asked, "Who touched me?" While all were denying it, Peter said, "Master, the crowds are pushing and pressing in upon you." Luke 8:45

I really hate the question. It puts me on the spot and makes my cerebral cortex work in overdrive, for an answer is needed immediately. The question is, "Do you remember me?"

Once you have been a priest in numerous parishes, the names and faces become a garbled mess. You will go to a store and see someone. You know you know them, but you're not sure if it's your dentist out of uniform or the groom of the couple you married ten years ago, or the person you met in the hospital at the death bed of their father. You know, however, they know you! It can be embarrassing not to remember parishioners you left behind.

I feel sorry for the staff and parishioners of a parish whose pastor is leaving. Moving a priest can be like a military operation. Similar to Operation Pack Up when the US left Iraq. The logistics takes coordination especially if the priest was at the parish for a long time. And then of course as one military operation is packing and leaving, another army is moving the new priest in. All within the same day, normally within hours.

First there is the sorting. A priest must be careful in sharing with his parishioners what he likes. Once they figure out he likes clowns or sail boats, he will collect enough clown figurines to fill a big top and enough sailboat paraphernalia to float an armada. All it takes is a casual comment in a homily about something, and the generosity of the people can be overwhelming.

Sometimes, I must admit, we priests use this to our advantage. For instance I know of priests (never me!) who likes to fish or hunt. They slyly bring a hunting or fishing story in a homily, kind of a way of trolling for an invitation, and suddenly after Mass they receive offers from parishioners who have land or ponds.

I don't think this is a bad thing. It's a manner of connecting and creating a relationship. I wonder what Jesus said in the synagogue giving Peter the idea first to invite Jesus over to his house for dinner (Luke 4:38). Jesus may have used meatloaf as an example in his preaching, and Peter's mother in law made a mean tasting meat loaf! Or perhaps Jesus casually said as a carpenter he had never fished in the Sea of Galilee, thus when Jesus asked to use Peter's boat, Peter invited Jesus to climb aboard. (Luke 5:3)

But when a priest moves, it provides him the opportunity to sort through these many treasures. Nonetheless then, what to do with them? I remember the story of a brother priest who graciously received a homemade fruitcake at the front door of the rectory. Fruitcake was on his "Most Hated List" of foods. So when he came into the rectory and a family was there who loved fruitcake, we saw it as the opportunity of grace.

That opportunity however turned to eating crow, when the recipient family inadvertently was seen by the donor, carrying the fruitcake out to the parking lot. So one must be careful of distributing one's gifts.

Then there is the awkwardness of finding things you thought were long lost. The piece of candy in the sweater pocket fusing the sweater pocket permanently shut. Or the small pile of unopened Christmas cards of several Christmas's past with generous gifts from loving parishioners. Or the photo of the young, good looking priest with a dapper moustache. Realizing it is a photo of you when you first arrived at the parish decades ago.

Finally there are the things you have no clue as to what to do with. The golf sticks you haven't used in ten years. The broken tennis racket. The yarn Mass vestments Matilda crocheted for you depicting rainbows and butterflies. Or the book series on "Amateur Taxidermy through the Bronze and Middle Ages" you were collecting (I love a series) but never read. These are the treasures a priest "leaves behind!"

Having moved into many rectories, I am amazed as to what a previous priest "leaves behind." Tee shirts, shoes, ugly Hawaiian shirts, gaudy coffee mugs, and of course ancient exercise equipment slightly used. And then often there is a surprise in the deep corner of the kitchen cupboard of a lost forgotten pickled something or other. (Feet are for walking, not pickling!) This is the category of what I call: "Let's leave this behind and I'll let the next guy worry about it!"

Thankfully my right frontal lobe allowed me to say to the former parishioner, "Yes, I remember you! You are Lauren!" With a huge smile and hug, I realized priests also leave something very important behind in parishes. The leave seeds of faith of the lives they touch. A treasure left behind.

22 YOU AREN'T GOING TO CHANGE ARE YOU???

"Jesus Christ is the same yesterday and today and forever." Hebrews 13:8

Getting into his car. A car of the 1980's, I was both anxious and excited. Not uneasy about his driving, but of our destination. Phoning a week or two prior to getting into his car, I asked for a ride. He remembers the call better than I.

"Hey, I'm Ken, and was accepted to the seminary. I understand you go to the same seminary. Can I have a ride with you?" Little did I understand this phone call would begin a brotherly relationship lasting until the present day.

"Sure," he said, "why don't you come over to my house, spend the night, and we can leave early the next morning."

I remember the car ride across town into a rural part of the county where he lived. Turning into the dirt road to his parent's home outside the city, it was situated on spacious land. Little did I know this spacious land would change me.

Change was a subject of conversation as I was preparing for the seminary adventure. I remember being asked, "You aren't going to change, are you?"

"What do you mean?" I replied.

"You aren't going to stop being yourself, are you?", was the response. I understood. They were afraid I would become no longer their brother, son, or friend. I don't think there was any danger of me suddenly becoming overly pious, but still, they understood this was a big step.

"No, I replied. I'll stay the same." And I meant it,....and God laughed.

Getting into my now new brother seminarian's car after the evening with his family, I was excited and at home. That was until I was given the rules of the car.

"Wipe your feet before you get in the car. No food and NO drinks. I want the inside to be clean!" he told me. 'No problem,' I thought, 'I can't blame him. It is a nice car. Big enough to fit a family of eight, but very nice.'

After five years in the seminary, and many trips back and forth with brother seminarians, I was finally ordained. I had only one request of the Lord in my first assignment. Okay, two. No big city parish and please don't make me follow a dynamic priest. And I meant it........and God laughed.

Assigned to the second largest parish in the diocese, and following a very popular dynamic priest, I soon settled into the routine of priesthood. Trying to "not be different" I soon found myself at odds with priestly life.

I was to experience the "first year" syndrome. Teachers, priests, and many other professionals go through it. Our first year or so, we try to be "the same" as we were before. We take on the new role of a priest or teacher and attempt to be everyone's friend. The same as before. We soon discover we cannot be what we were.

I recall my first "days off" as a priest. I would get into my blue jeans and shirt and think, "Now, I can be ME!" Relaxing one day off at a Kansas lake in my "ME" attire, I heard a voice behind tentatively saying, "Father Ken????"

"Yes," I cautiously replied.

"I heard you would be here. I live in a nearby town, and I was wondering if you could help me with my annulment papers?" And so for the next couple of weeks, on my day off, in "ME attire," I helped him with his papers.

I soon learned, I had changed, even though I didn't feel changed. That would come later.

There was once a man born blind. Anointed with mud made from Jesus' saliva, he washed and was healed of his blindness. Seeing, but still the same person, he couldn't understand why his friends and neighbors did not recognize him. Only after recognizing Jesus as the Son of God, did he recognize why he was different. He was the same, yet different. (John 9)

Getting into my brother priest's truck, I had to move some cups, papers, tools, and a few other items cluttering the passenger side in order to find space to sit. "You've changed since we first rode to the seminary together decades ago." I teased him.

"Yes," he said, "I don't know why I was so particular then. I guess my priorities have changed."

Driving past the spacious land which once held the home we left on our journey to the seminary, I looked directly across the street. There sits one of the largest Catholic parishes. Built here because of widening highway. A church and people whom I had the privilege to shepherd and father through the sorrow of tearing one holy structure down, and building a new one.

Reflecting on those early days of the priesthood, and recognizing the "ME "in me has become the "Christ" for us, I feel changed. Hoping I never have to go through such changes again, I realize I really mean it....and I can hear God chuckle.

23 DON'T REACH UNDER THERE!!!

"Israel their father then told them: "If it must be so, then do this: Put some of the land's best products in your baggage and take them down to the man as gifts: some balm and honey, gum and resin, and pistachios and almonds." Genesis 43:11

"Come to him, a living stone, rejected by human beings but chosen and precious in the sight of God," 1 Peter 2:4

As a young priest I found it difficult to sit in the Confessional in such a confined space. Now I love it. I often think of the Trappist author Michael Casey who

wrote 'that which brings the young man to the door of the monastery, will not be the reason he remains in the monastery." How true.

When a man and woman enter sacramental marriage they overlook the distasteful traits of one another. Soon however, these traits can no longer remain hidden and must either be gotten rid of or accepted. What couples often find is the longer they are married, either these little things become more irritating, or they become accepted and even grown fond of.

Growing up I remember my father's sneeze. For some reason, he couldn't just sneeze once. No, it was a series of at least seven sneezes. Rather irritating and very embarrassing when I was around my neighborhood friends. But then one summer I was far away from home, and by myself, when I overheard another man rapid fire sneezes. I was comforted by those irritating sneezes, and looked forward to getting home and hearing them from my father.

Sitting in a confined confession was like an irritating habit of a spouse or parent for me. At first I struggled with sitting and hearing confessions. But now, it has become the most welcomed part of my priesthood. At the end of the day, when I wonder if attending meetings, answering e-mails, and returning phone calls is what a priest is about, all I have to do is remember my time during the day sitting in the confessional. I am comforted knowing I sat there forgiving sins. Then whatever else I did that day would pale in comparison.

One evening after the Saturday evening Confessions, I decided to settle into a pew of the church. I love this time of day in the church. The lingering remnants of parishioners remain in the atmosphere and air of the church. Often I'll sit in different parts of the church remembering which parishioner or family normally sits there, and offer intercessory prayers for them.

Settling this night into the pew, I could feel the warm presence of our Lord enfolding around me. It was then I grasped the seat portion of the pew to adjust my seating when my fingers felt under the pew. I could feel small nodules attached to the wood. Most were hard, but some soft. Like barnacles on the bottom of a ship, I instantly realized what my fingers sank into. ABC Gum! (Already Been Chewed Gum)

Gum, that soft, cohesive substance made for chewing but not swallowing, peppered the underneath side of the pew. Chewing gum has been used by humans since the time of King David, some 3000 years ago, and from the look of it, we had about 3000 years' worth of gum under the pew.

It doesn't take much to distract me in prayer, but gushy, sticky, probably germ filled gum between my fingers will definitely do it! Returning from the restroom after cleaning my hands, I realized the gum under the pews would need to be removed at some point.

Settling into the pew again and regaining my composure before the Eucharistic Lord, I wondered just how much gum was under all these pews, and if we scraped the gum off, would the pews still stand? It was then the Lord was smiling at me and inspired me with the thought: "That filthy, sticky gum you are finding is like sin, and the church is the best place to leave it!"

I realized He was right. Often we come to church to receive, but in fact what the Lord wants us to do is to leave. Leave Him our sins and our worries; our weaknesses and filth. They say gum will not remain in your stomach for seven years if you swallow it, but it sure feels nasty when you do swallow it! Kind of like our sins.

So the next time you are in your parish church and you reach under the pew and touch the gum barnacles, think of them as your sins you have left in the Confessional with the priest who is Christ. A perfect place to deposit them. What a wonderful reminder.

Perhaps I won't clean under the pews after all.

24 SIGNS, SIGNS, EVERYWHERE SIGNS!

"You brought your people Israel out of the land of Egypt with signs and wonders, with a strong hand and an

outstretched arm, and great terror." Jeremiah 32:21

"The signs of an apostle were performed among you with all endurance, signs and wonders, and mighty deeds." 2 Corinthians 12:12

Twenty! Yes, that's right! There were no less than 20 signs in the parish kitchen! There were signs about how to turn on the garbage disposal; what could and could not be disposed.

Other signs instructed who could use the refrigerator and what is to be stored, as well as how each item should be labeled with a sign.

There were signs about how doors opened doors, what cabinets could not be used, who could use of pots/pans, and procedures of locking and unlocking. Some were gentle reminders and others were demanding.

There is always a story behind each sign, so when I read them, I question what happened to create the sign. For instance, the sign stating: "Place no kids in the ice maker." Perhaps someone thought children are better-behaved after you lower their core body temperature.

Or the sign over a trash can which read, "Do not throw forks in trash." When I asked, a parishioner said perhaps the forks poked holes in the trash bags. What about knives? They weren't sure. Must be a story behind it.

Signs have always been an important way of communication in our spiritual history. Often God used signs to communicate a message to us. "Then Gideon said to God, "If you are truly going to use me to rescue Israel as you promised, prove it to me in this way. I will put a wool fleece on the threshing floor tonight. If the fleece is wet with dew in the morning but the ground is dry, then I will know that you are going to help me rescue Israel as you promised." And that is just what happened..." (Judges 6: 36-38)

Or when "God said to Noah .... When the bow appears in the clouds, I will see it and remember the everlasting covenant between God and every living creature—every mortal being that is on earth." (Genesis 9: 8-16)

Signs are confirmations, usually of God's providential care for His loved ones. But signs can also be used differently.

He was newly ordained. I was an older priest and his pastor, far beyond his age by at least four years! Okay, so we both were pretty much newly ordained, but I still was pastor. There were certain things I needed to teach my new young curate, but didn't want to overwhelm him by nagging him constantly. "Things" such as what temperature the thermostat should be set in the sacristy; how chalices should be placed in the cabinet (kind of like Tupperware, they have to go a certain way to fit!); or how to hang the stoles on the chasuble hanger so they don't get wrinkled (yeah, only a priest worries about this one).

So how to instruct and yet not admonish? Tutor and not reprimand? Basically how to get him to do what I wanted him to do??? I came up with the perfect idea! Post It Notes!!! Starting in just a few areas, I placed instructional notes of what to do and what not to do. It seemed to work. I conveyed my desire but didn't have to confront. Perfect!

But like mold, once it got a foot hold, it spread. Soon the little yellow Post It Notes became larger multi-colored Post It Notes which seem to replicate on their own. Soon the sacristy resembled a patchwork quilt. This Joseph of Many Coats soon spread to other parts of the parish: the working sacristy, the rectory, the kitchen, and finally the garage.

He was patient, I'll give him that! But at some point there must have been a tipping point, because in the sacristy one morning he exploded. "Why are you leaving me all these little notes?" He exclaimed. "Why can't you just talk to me? I know English you know!" (Not his first language)

Therapists say some people try to exert control over others by putting up instructional or reprimanding signs, but instead of creating cohesive behavior, it becomes derisive and childish. Taking down my many signs, I realized simply talking is the best communication tool.

However sometimes signs are helpful, such as the "signs of the fig tree," (Luke 21:28) or signs of power (John 20:30). But the most important sign we have received is sign of the cross and resurrection. This is the one "sign" we should adorn every room and aspect of our life.

Looking around the parish kitchen as I was leaving, another sign over a very large red button caught my attention. It said, "If you don't know what this button is for, LEAVE IT ALONE!"

I left it alone, but boy was it tempting! Perhaps a sign that I am growing up and becoming wiser?

25 WISHING I WAS SOMEONE ELSE

"But you are a chosen race, a royal priesthood, a holy nation, a people for his own possession, that you may proclaim the excellences of him who called you out of darkness into his marvelous light." 1 Peter 2:9

My mind was where it should not have been. I felt adrift, feeling unappreciated and invisible. It had been a long day.

In writing about the experience of living the Catholic priesthood, I am often surprised how readers will share amazement that priests have similar struggles as they. This is a tactic of the devil. Encouraging us to believe others have it all together,  all the time. I am quite convinced most of us, priest and lay, have it together only a small portion of the time and are good performers the rest of the time.

My mind was reflecting upon the undertakings of my day and was entering into the evening responsibilities. Questioning not my vocation, but whether I was being truthful to my calling. As with all of our vocations, whether celibate or married, living in the world or cloistered, we will often question our decisions made in initial fervor. With age, we reminisce on what we would have done differently and how to be faithful to what we began.

Looking up, I could see they were lost. I could tell it, and they didn't know it.

In my dark thoughts, I was walking between the priest residences and the diocesan retreat center and I saw a car filled with young men outfitted in suit and ties. Hesitating at the entrance of the complex, first turning one direction, then with a speed only a young driver can suddenly make, turned the other direction.

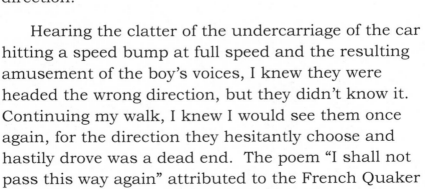

Hearing the clatter of the undercarriage of the car hitting a speed bump at full speed and the resulting amusement of the boy's voices, I knew they were headed the wrong direction, but they didn't know it. Continuing my walk, I knew I would see them once again, for the direction they hesitantly choose and hastily drove was a dead end. The poem "I shall not pass this way again" attributed to the French Quaker missionary Stephen Grellet would not be their song.

Minutes later, the tune "Here we go again," was in

my mind as the car filled with these young men raced back towards me after completing their dead end destination. Pulling to a quick stop, I leaned down to the open window and asked, "Are you looking for the Bishop's house?"

"Yes," they breathlessly said, as if they were running instead of riding in an automobile. "We are supposed to have dinner with him tonight. We can't find it!"

After giving quick directions to the Bishop's house, they spun off. I suspected they didn't really hear my instructions, but at least now they were headed in the right direction and would eventually find their way to the Bishop's home.

The bishop was hosting a dinner for young men who might be interested in becoming priests. It was an opportunity for him to get to know prospective seminarians, and for these young men to become familiar with their bishop in a more casual setting. As they raced off, I began to feel somewhat jealous of not being their age and as untroubled.

The young men brought my mind out of itself and my review of the long day, but now I returned to my dark thoughts. It was a day in council meetings, listening to concerns, working through employee matters, and of course more meetings.

I ruminated on the columnist Dave Barry's words, "If you had to identify, in one word, the reason why the human race has not achieved its full potential, that word would be 'meetings.'" 'Am I really doing what you want, Lord?' I prayed, 'Is this my full potential?'

Hearing the boys' laughter behind me as they again hit the speed bump at full speed, Our Lord gently said, "They want what you have. They want to be you!"

"Huh?!?" I reply (A proper response to the Lord. Not what Mary would have responded, but probably more like Joseph's reply). 'Why would they want to be me?' I asked the Lord. He simply smiled. (I get that answer a lot from Him. That and chuckling.)

My mind was then set into motion. 'They want to be me. Here I was wanting to be them....why would they want to be me?' Reviewing my day once again, the Lord quietly but firmly helped me see it through different lenses. Not only was my day filled with meetings, it was also composed of another litany. As a priest today I forgave sins, consecrated bread and wine into the Body and Blood of Jesus, and brought the healing presence of Jesus to the sick, counseled, instructed, and prayed in a way only a priest could, i.e., in His name, and as Him: in persona Christi.

I now understood why someone would want to be me, or rather be who I am and Who I bring. Like the boys, I then made a turnaround, although in spirit, for I too was lost and didn't know it, and He pointed me in the right direction. Now, I just need to be sure to slow down for those speed bumps I sometimes find at the end of a long day.

26 BELIEF IN SPITE OF OUR FAILURES

But he said to me, "My grace is sufficient for you, for my power is made perfect in weakness." Therefore I will boast all the more gladly of my weaknesses, so that the power of Christ may rest upon me." 2 Corinthians 12:9

I could tell he did not believe me. His head was cocked to one side, twisting in a way to see me eye to eye. I told him I would be coming back. Even gave him a snack, but I could tell he did not believe me.

Preparing for a short trip, I was packing my luggage while my faithful pup of a dog was accompanying me in the bedroom as I sorted through my clothing for the trip. "Ahh, what color black should I wear 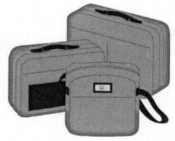 this trip," I was thinking to myself. "Should I wear the faded black shirt, or I guess they call it stonewashed today? Or should I wear the dark black hue shirt which was brand new?" Before becoming a priest, I had no idea there were different "colors" of black. Such fashion decisions wear me out, so I sat down to pet my pup....he knew something was up. Treats and luggage means he won't be seeing me for a while.

When one thinks of the being a steward of God's gifts we generally think of the blessings we receive. But do we consider the tragic events of our lives as blessings also? I doubt it. When Jesus climbed the mountain and gathered his disciples around him and he began to teach the Beatitudes, I wonder if the disciples and crowd cocked their heads from side to side like my pup did to me. How could tragedy be a blessing? Why would we want to be a steward of misfortune?

Oftentimes when I preach, I use examples from fields of work or circumstances of living of which I have no experience. Jesus did the same thing. Jesus was a carpenter, yet he spoke of fishing, farming, and shepherding. Common examples of the life in His era, but not of His life experiences. However, I have learned not to use child birthing in my homilies as the prophet Isaiah (Isaiah 42). When I do try, I normally get scowls from women which say, "You really don't know what you are talking about!"

Can misfortunes and confusion be a gift from the Lord? Do we really believe from hardship come success? Often we believe such gifts in the secular or business world. For example, Walt Disney was fired by a newspaper editor because the editor thought Walt lacked imagination and had no good ideas. Or poor Albert Einstein who was expelled from school. Or the poor truck driver who in 1954 the manager of the Grand Ole Opry told him to go back to truck driving, because "you ain't going nowhere son!" That of course, was Elvis Presley.

So If we believe misfortune can lead to success in the secular world, what about the spiritual world? Are these beatitudes all they seem to be? Saint Augustine famously said, "There is no saint without a past, and no sinner without a future."

Thomas J. Craughwell, the author of "Saints Behaving Badly" writes of several saints who first failed in the spiritual life, only then to succeed. Saints such as Angela of Foligno who was canonized by Pope Francis. Angela spent most of her life seeking wealth, material possessions, and pleasure. She was married with children, but was more interested in acquiring wealth and status then caring for her family.

Then around the age of 40, she had a profound conversion experience. She realized how her desire and pursuit for worldly things left her in spiritual poverty. Her life was completely empty of joy and life. It was only when Angela was empty the Lord could fill her. Pope Benedict XVI said of Angela that "God has a thousand ways, for each of us, to make Himself present in the soul, to show that He exists and knows and loves me." Pope Benedict credits Angela's continued conversion to her prayer life.

Priests are in need of conversion too. Many parishioners are surprised at this. Generally in a priest's life, prior to becoming a seminarian, there is a moment of conversion gently pushing him to accept the Lord's invitation to enter studies for the priesthood. But like Angela or Teresa of Avila, conversion must continue past the initial fervor.

"Do you know Father B?" a man asked me at dinner. I am always amazed people don't realize we diocesan priests in a diocese know each other. We are brothers, working and living together. After acknowledging I knew my brother priest, he said, "He is REALLY holy!" I agreed with him, which must have made him uncomfortable, so he followed it up with, "I suppose you are holy too in your own way."

Yes, I suppose so, although, I seem to hide it from most people! In reflecting upon the holiness of my brother priest, I am also aware of his failings. I know he would be the last person in the world who would consider himself holy. Walking with him through some difficult times in his life, I can clearly see who he is today, is because of his struggles of the past. He could proclaim like Saint Paul, "I will all the more gladly boast of my weaknesses, that the power of Christ may rest upon me." (2 Corinthians 12:9)

Saints are not born saints, they are made. Even Saint Joseph struggled. Matthew records in his first chapter how Mary and Joseph were betrothed, but Mary was found to be with child of the Holy Spirit. Joseph's response? He resolved to send her away quietly. (Mt. 1:19) He struggled with believing Mary. So much so, God graced him with a dream in which Joseph was assured of the truth of what Mary was saying.

You might think since Joseph received a dream, all would we well, and he could trust such action as being from the Lord. Not necessary. Another man, whose wife had a dream, ignored it. (Mt. 27:19) That man was Pontius Pilate. So Joseph, like Pontius Pilate, had to make a choice, and act of the will, to believe or not to believe.

The Beatitudes are sometimes hard to believe. The Gospel sometimes seems too good to be true, and we might cock our head from side to side, wanting to get a view of Jesus eye to eye, just to make sure. Conversion is about trust. Not in a philosophy, but in a person. We put our trust in Jesus who said, I am the living bread which came down from heaven; if any one eats of this bread, he will live forever; and the bread which I shall give for the life of the world is my flesh." (John 6:51) Of which our response is, "Lord to whom shall we go? You have the words of eternal life." (John 6:68)

A priest can learn a lot by being a steward of his blessings, but also of his weaknesses and failures. "We know that in everything, God works for good with those who love Him..." (Romans 8:28)

27 MENTORING VERSES NURTURING

"Then the Lord God said, "It is not good that the man should be alone; I will make him a helper fit for him." Genesis 2:18

Slowly they came forward. Years of pastoral experience. The wisdom etched on their faces was revealed in the evening light shining through the chapel windows. As the prayers of the Church were prayed over them, a priest, many years younger than they, placed his hands on their bowed heads. The older priests then extended their hands, slowly turning their palms toward the chapel floor, allowing the younger priest to anoint the backsides of their hands with holy oil, the oil of the infirmed, and pray for healing.

Every year priests of a diocese gather together to make a spiritual retreat. These retreats are attended by the newly ordained and the newly retired. Within the retreat are opportunities for priests to minister to one another through the sacrament of Holy Communion, Confession, but most visibly in the Anointing of the Sick.

This visible ministering of a bishop to his priests, or of a youthful energetic newly ordained priest to his elders, is one of the most poignant examples of the words of Jesus, "Take my yoke upon you and learn from me, for I am meek and humble of heart...." (Matthew 11:29) In it is found the passing on of the faith from one generation to another, from one priest to another.

I quickly learned to make my own opinion. I was told this older priest was conservative. I chuckled at this impression of my brother priest of my new pastor as I placed the pastor's Waterford crystal chalice on the altar. (It was the 80's and crystal chalices were still allowed) I knew I would learn much from this man, as I spied the many books on healing and of the Charismatic movement on his book shelves, along with the encyclicals of the great popes. He was a man of his times. Ordained before Vatican Council II and ministering after.

The idea was for this man to mentor me into the priesthood. It didn't happen that way. When one mentors another, the idea is to advise and train,

especially a younger colleague. This learning partnership is between a person with vast experience and someone who wants to learn. Perhaps there lay the problem. He had much experience, but I was not necessarily wanting to always learn.

It was in high school I seriously considered not attending college. I was the same child who after kindergarten thought we were done. In many ways I was probably correct, but nonetheless, they sent me to grade school anyway. Entering college with similar expectations, I ended up on a five year college plan. A "five year college plan" for many means starting in one area of study, only to change it in midstream, lengthening your studies and costs.

After my five year college career, I felt called to the priesthood much to the dismay of my girlfriend. "Hard to fight God," she would later tell me. So after an additional five years in the seminary, I was quite ready to be the teacher, not the learner. Therefore when assigned a parish and pastor as a deacon, the final step to priesthood, I was not ready to be mentored.

It was a good thing my new pastor for the summer was not at a place in his life or priesthood to mentor a young man. He was at the end of a long and illustrious priesthood. As a military chaplain, pastor, and most of all a man of great faith, he was either too tired to mentor me, or too wise to do so. No, instead of "mentoring" he "nurtured."

"Ken, please come to my office," he asked me. When I showed up, he took a good look at me, shuffled some papers on his desk, puffed his pipe, and then said, "I guess if I ask you to come to my office, I should have something profound to tell you." I wasn't sure how to respond, but he went on to say after a rather long pause in which he was trying find something profound to say, "Well, how are you doing?"

He wasn't sure how to "mentor" me, but he was good at nurturing. Over the dinner table he reminded me why my mother taught me how to eat like a gentleman, for I was in the presence of a real gentleman who ate with etiquette and style. In the afternoon he showed me how to live a balanced life, as I would watch him in his old farmer's clothing water the many trees he had planted throughout the parish campus. Slowly from tree to tree, he would give water to the roots of these newly planted trees. "A time of reflection" he would say.

At least once a week he would display to me the importance of play in a man's life. Coming to my room with plaid shorts and a golf hat, we would hit the links of the local golf course. All the while talking about life, the church or parish, and most of all how to keep from slicing the ball.

Finally, it was hearing the back screen door slam at 6:55am every morning that nurtured me. The slam of the outer screen door would signal the beginning of his day as he headed off to the Adoration Chapel for an hour of adoration before the Blessed Sacrament.

Only a few can mentor, but all of us can nurture. We nurture one another, not with great expertise, but with authentically living our lives in the manner in which we believe God is asking. The greatest act of nurturing my deaconate pastor gave me was when in his retirement, he returned home to allow others to serve his spiritual and physical needs.

So when I saw them slowly coming forward with years of pastoral experience etched on their faces and hands, I realized the difference between mentoring and nurturing, and how our Lord calls us to primarily nurture one another. It was in their hands.

Deliberately they lifted up their hands. Hands which lifted up chalices and consecrated hosts, babies to be baptized, rings to be blessed. Hands which administrated with pens and computers and ministered with bread, wine, and oils. Lifting up their hands, they slowly turned them over, palms down, surrendering the backsides of their hands to be anointed by a younger, more vigorous priest to bless their hands with oil and pray for healing of body and spirit.

This act of total surrender to the Father through a younger priest is an act of nurturing. One in which we are all called to do. Only a few can mentor, but all of us can nurture. *"Father into your hands I commend my spirit."* (Luke 23:46)

28 THE THREE CANCERS OF THE PRIESTHOOD

"You shall serve the Lord your God, and he will bless your bread and your water, and I will take sickness away from among you." Exodus 23:25

He had an energy about him that was contagious. Newly ordained, the oils, as we say among priests, were not yet dry. He had a glow about him. I rather disliked him for it.

Recently I was speaking with another priest. We had attended the seminary together. Adding up the years we had ministered and figuring how many more we had in "active" ministry, we realized we were past the middle point of our ministry. Priests "retire" at 75 although often a priest can petition to retire at 70.

I think such discussions are called "Middle Aged Discussions." We have not moved to the "What All

Physically Ails You Discussion." Or the comparison of medical procedures at the lunch table. That will come soon enough. No, at this point, we are between two movements of life: the sending forth, and the being called home.

It is great fun to be at this juncture in one's life. We look at the young priests through the wisdom of middle age seeing what they are doing, knowing we probably still have the energy, but wise enough to know we don't have to as Saint Ignatius of Loyola would say, "inflammate omnia—"Go, set the world on fire."

As I watch our young priests, first of all, it is amazing we have so many young priests! When I was in the seminary in the 1980's, we were often reminded of how it was in the past, when the seminaries were full after the Second World War. What a springtime of vocations we are currently experiencing.

Having been a pastor of several large parishes, I had the privilege of having numerous associates. Over ten I counted up. I suspect they gather on a regular basis as a self-help group. I can see them gathered: "Hi, I am Father So and So, and I was an associate of Father Ken!"

These associates came in many different theological flavors and human personalities. Each unique. The greatest mistake I made with these young men was not realizing their particular uniqueness, or giftedness. I saw them as another member of the staff, filling a spot vacated by the previous associate. Similar to replacing a secretary. From one secretary to another, their skill sets would be similar, if not the same.

Priests however, do not necessarily have the same "skill sets." Saint Paul wrote, "To each individual the manifestation of the Spirit is given for some benefit. To one...wisdom, to another knowledge..., another healing....another mighty deeds...another prophecy..." (See 1 Corinthians 12:7-11)

Using Saint Paul's words, the same could be said of associates and pastors. "To each associate (or pastor) the manifestation of the Spirit given through ordination is given for some benefit. To one priest administrative skills, to another youth ministry. To another gentleness in face of illness, to another patience and skill of running a meeting."

It wasn't until I grew more mature and wiser, when I realized the associate was not here to primarily serve the parish, but rather the parish was there to serve the young priest by forming him, encouraging him to discover his gifts, and simply being Christ to them.

A healthy group of priests will have both young and old. But in such a mix, the enemy can become present. Saint Paul was writing to a young priest, Timothy, giving him advice about being young: "Don't let anyone look down on you because you are young...." 1 Timothy 4:12. Or when Paul wrote to young preacher Titus when he gave a warning about old men: "older men are to be temperate, dignified, sensible, sound in faith, in love in perseverance." Titus 2:2.

Why these warnings and advice among the priests? Whether it is post World War, present day, or in the future, our priests can be likened to the Apostles. Yes, we have been given the sacramental authority to forgive sins (John 20:23). We have the privilege of leaving all and following Jesus (Matthew 20:21).

We also have the honor of being in a special relationship with Mary, the Mother of God.

Unfortunately, what we sometimes have in common with the Apostles is not the authority or special relationships with Jesus and Mary; rather we have what might be called, "Apostolic weaknesses." Or as our Bishop Emeritus Gerber called, "The three cancers of the priesthood." They are: to compare, compete, and complain.

"They came to Capernaum and, once inside the house, he began to ask them, "What were you arguing about on the way?" But they remained silent. They had been discussing among themselves on the way who was the greatest. (Mark 9: 33-34)

Let's explore these weaknesses or cancers, knowing they are not exclusive to the ministerial ordained priesthood, but all Christians by virtue of their baptism have been included into the priesthood of Christ, and therefore also struggle with these weaknesses.

29 THE THREE CANCERS OF THE PRIESTHOOD
NUMBER ONE: COMPARING

"Heal the sick, raise the dead, cleanse lepers, cast out demons. You received without paying; give without pay." Matthew 10:8

It didn't take much. It was a casual comment, but it was the glow in the eyes that bothered me the most. A parishioner caught me in the Gathering Space of the church.

This space is a place for parishioners to gather before or after Mass. Much goes on in this space, whether it is a large or small space. Whether it is really the size of a lobby or vestibule, or whether you can "stack a whole lot of hay in it" as one rancher told me, it is a space for the Body of Christ to assemble.

Ideally it is a liturgical space where processions begin. Here the bride and groom gather in a procession to begin a life together. Or a grieving family will assemble with the body of their loved one to say a final earthly farewell. It is also the place where every Sunday Mass begins, commonly with the "priestly wave" from the back of the church signaling to the cantor or lector to announce the opening hymn.

While it is a liturgical area, one must also realize it is used for other purposes such as a place to distribute the Altar Society raffle tickets for a quilt everyone wants, but is too beautiful to really use for sleeping, or the place to display those high caloric Girl Scout cookies or gluten free Boy Scout popcorn.

And let's not forget it is also a parade ground for children. As soon as Mass begins, the Privy Pied Piper begins his tune, and in unison every ambulatory child through their teen 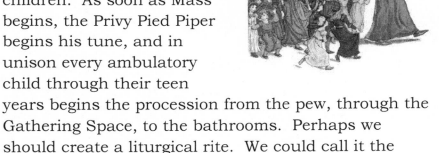 years begins the procession from the pew, through the Gathering Space, to the bathrooms. Perhaps we should create a liturgical rite. We could call it the "Convoy to the Commode" ritual. It usually begins with the Gloria, and ends during the first verse of the final hymn.

Of course the ritual includes what I call the Family Circus Rite. The child first goes to the restroom, but upon exiting begins a trajectory towards the bulletin board. After reading about all the job opportunities, they head over to the lost and found box. After opening the umbrellas and looking at car keys left behind wondering how the parishioner got home, the child of God begins a trail back to the pew. Only after dousing themselves with Holy Water in the re-baptism ritual.

Generally I try to sprint through the "gathering space." For me, it's a place for me to "gather" my thoughts as I am in route either to or from the sacristy but on this particular day I almost tripped over a parishioner who I could see had something to tell me.

"Oh Father! I'm so glad I ran into you." She said, although I knew she was secretly waiting in ambush. Some parishioners are as patient as duck hunters on opening day of the season. This particular parishioner used the American flag in the Gathering Space as her duck blind, I literally almost ran into her, as she came forth from her priest hunting blind.

"Oh, I just had to tell you," she continued, "I was over at Saint Edmund the Martyr parish, and Father O'Malley gave the most inspiring homily!" A twenty gauge shotgun could have done no less damage to my ego than those words! Such an accurate shot for a wide spread weapon!

My mind begins to race...'Where did you come from?....You're MY parishioner, why were you at Father O'Malley's Mass....I must have done something wrong because obviously you quit the parish and joined St. Edmund's...No, you're still here, so you must be still my parishioner....'

Then, the mind really goes…. 'Father O'Malley gave an inspiring homily?....I went to school with him, and he slept through most of it, or played golf….really, O'Malley??? I wonder why you are telling me this….OH! Your telling me, my homilies are terrible!....Why should I care, you can't even stay in one parish for Mass!'

Perhaps it's a male thing. "When David returned from killing the Philistine, the women came out of all the cities of Israel, singing and dancing, to meet King

 Saul, playing songs of joy on timbrels. The women sang as they played, and said, "Saul has killed his thousands, and David his ten thousands." Then Saul became very angry. This saying did not please him. He said, "They have given David honor for ten thousands, but for me only thousands. Now what more can he have but to be king?" And Saul was jealous and did not trust David from that day on." (1 Samuel 18:6-9)

One of the great cancers among us priests is comparing ourselves to other priests. "An argument arose among the disciples about which of them was the greatest…" Luke 9:48. It's nothing new, but gets really old after a while. You would think we would eventually grow up.

This was not my first time I contracted this cancer. Early in my priesthood, I contracted this comparing disease. At that time I contracted due to an older priest. He was my senior by at least 20 years, yet he could run circles around me. I called him an energizer bunny! After four Masses on Sunday, he then would baptize children and go to their parents' home.

Later he would go to the retreat house for the closing ceremony of a retreat, only then to come home after visiting someone in the hospital. Then I would find him with paperwork spread out all over the living room while he watched the last of a baseball game into the wee hours of the night.

I tried. I really tried, but I couldn't keep up with him. After the Masses on Sunday, I was already pretty much worn-out and dragged myself to the youth ministry for a short time. That was enough for me! But I thought I needed to be more active, more available, a better priest. Since I couldn't keep up, I felt like a failure.

We know the Holy Spirit gives different gifts to individuals, but we erroneously think every priest should at least have a set of basic gifts from the Holy Spirit. It took me a long time in pursuing these gifts, only to realize it is not true. The pursuit of these basic gifts of the Holy Spirit, led me to the second "C", or cancer of the priesthood: competition.

30 THE THREE CANCERS OF THE PRIESTHOOD
NUMBER TWO: COMPETITION

"At the approach of Saul and David, on David's return after striking down the Philistine, women came out from all the cities of Israel to meet Saul the king, singing and dancing, with tambourines, joyful songs, and stringed instruments. The women played and sang:

"Saul has slain his thousands, David his tens of thousands."

Saul was very angry and resentful of the song, for he thought: "They give David tens of thousands, but only thousands to me. All that remains for him is the kingship." From that day on, Saul kept a jealous eye on David." 1 Samuel 18:6-9

It was more than 60, but less than 100. After 25 years, I forget, but at the time, we counted each step. The seminary I attended did not have an elevator to the fifth floor. In fact, it had no elevator until about my second or third year in the seminary. The stair case was an open stair case. Now, I would imagine due to fire codes, it has been enclosed.

An open stair case allows several things. It allows a seminarian to drop his dirty laundry bag down five building floors into the basement after yelling "Dirty laundry. Look out below!" One learns very quickly at the seminary never to look over the banister unless you want to lose your head with dirty laundry. Imagine the phone call to your parents..."Yes; your son was injured by smelly clothes." An open stair case also allows those at the bottom of the building to hear who won the competition between two brother seminarians, racing up the ten flights of stairs, counting each step, and the announcement of the winner at the top!

Perhaps it was at this junction the second cancer of the priesthood began. The first cancer is found inside one's mind, that is comparing yourself to other seminarians/priests. This cancer is always followed by a more active tumor called, competition. Again, maybe it's a male thing, but once you begin to compare your priesthood against another priest, and falling short, the progression of the disease will be competition against the brother priest.

He didn't know it, but I had won. I was speaking with a new parishioner, completing paperwork for the baptism of their fifth child. I had seen this family for some time at Mass because they were one of my hyphenated parishioners.

A "hyphenated parishioner" is a family who vacillates between two different neighboring parishes. They are registered in one parish but because of convenience of Mass times, family ties, or the personality of the priest, they attend Mass at the neighboring parish often. Upon hearing at the meeting with the parishioners they were finally letting go of the "hyphen" and registering in my parish, I felt smug and quite superior to my brother priest.

"Oh Father," the wife said, "We have been coming to YOUR parish for some time, and find YOUR liturgies and YOUR homilies so inspiring and so we decided to join YOUR parish."

Instead of replying as our Lord did, "Get behind me you Satan!" (Matthew 10:16) when He recognized a parishioner (Peter) stroking His ego rather than seeing and accepting as God sees and accepts, I was inwardly pleased. I won! I beat my brother priest in proclaiming the Gospel of Jesus Christ! I was a better priest, more compassionate, more down to earth, more Christ like, more holy! I was the winner of a contest he didn't know he was competing in.

"Since you have an associate priest here, we were wondering if you wouldn't mind if we called each week to get the schedule of when YOUR Masses are, so we wouldn't have to attend his?" Now I even accomplished defeating my newly ordained associate! Wow, am I good!

God always gives us what we need, when we need it, although sometimes we would rather refuse it! My "it" was after scheduling the baptism with my new flattering parishioners, I was out of town the weekend of the baptism. A scheduling mix up on my part. My young associate baptized their child. Afterwards, I ran into the family after Mass the following weekend in the Gathering Space, and I was rather bewildered.

They were leaving Mass. A Mass that I did not celebrate. A Mass my young associate celebrated. Huh? Thinking they were upset I was unable to baptize their child, I began to apologize for the mix up, when the wife interrupted me by saying, "Oh Father, that's okay! Father Mathias did a wonderful job! We just LOVE him! He came over after the baptism and joined the family in dinner, and then he played football with the children. Wow, what energy! He really relates to the children. They LOVE him and want to go to HIS Masses! You are so blessed to have him as YOUR associate!"

Yes, I was thinking as they left. And I'll bet he can run up five flights of stairs without gasping for breath too! A good lesson for me. Eventually I didn't see this particular family any more. I suspect another dashing priest caught their attention and they were off following HIS Masses. I cannot fault the family, for we priests, in the midst our competition for attention, create such a climate. If only we could learn sooner, it's all for the honor and glory of God. It's not about us! I felt like the people of Galatia whom Saint Paul reprimanded in Galatians 3:1. (You have look it up!)

Time can eliminate the need for competition. Now I feel successful when I can walk up two flights of stairs without having to stop and catch my breath, let alone run up the stairs in competition of another priest. I don't need to compete with anyone now, I am just trying to take care of myself and get up the flight of stairs.

Perhaps the saying familiar to all priests is fulfilled with this passage of time: "When I was newly ordained, I was going to save the world. As I got older, I just wanted to save my parish. Now that I am even older, all I can do is try and save myself."

Competition blinds us to the fact only Our Lord does the saving. We are simply to remove the plank from our eyes, so He can use us to help others. If one doesn't grow beyond competing with another, the final cancer will present itself, and it's the worst, most visible of all of the "C's." It is complaining.

31 THE THREE CANCERS OF THE PRIESTHOOD NUMBER THREE: COMPLAINING

"Be hospitable to one another without complaining." 1 Peter 4:9

"Boy, that was a waste of time!" I told a brother priest, as we were leaving a meeting. Father Ronald Rolheiser wrote a wonderful article once entitled, "Pentecost happened at a meeting." In my mind, if the Holy Spirit showed up at the meeting we just finished, the Holy Spirit would have fallen asleep like the young man who fell slumbered during a sermon by Saint Paul and fell out of a window. (Think your pastor gives long and boring homilies? Go to Acts 20:9 and see that even saints sometimes went too long!)

As we continued to walk my complaints became more numerous about the meeting's agenda, the participants, and the leadership. I even complained about the coffee! Becoming more boisterous and loud, I suddenly was silenced, as I glanced behind me, I saw the leader of the meeting walking silently behind us.

Not sure what was overheard, but presuming everything was heard, I quickly made an exit to my car. The drive home was long for me. I kept thinking what Bishop Emeritus Gerber said, "A grateful heart silences a complaining tongue."

The three cancers of the priesthood: compare, compete, and complain are shared by all of humanity, but grows particularly abhorrent in the ordained priesthood. I, who have been ordained by God for the service of the People of God, should of all people, be a person of gratitude. For my complaints about meetings, brother priests, parishioners, even the weather, are really complaints against He who made it all.

"Moses said, 'When the Lord gives you in the evening meat to eat and in the morning bread to the full, because the Lord has heard your grumbling that you grumble against him...what are we? Your grumbling is not against us, but against the Lord." Exodus 16:8

In a driver's education book, a warning sign is defined as "These signs warn of dangerous or unusual conditions ahead such as a curve,

turn, dip, or side road. They are usually diamond-shaped and have a yellow background letters or symbols."

This third cancer, complaining, is a warning sign that the other two tumors are present: comparing and competing. Anytime I am conscious of complaining, it's a warning sign to me of a dangerous condition meaning I am already comparing and competing. I am going down a side road which I may never return. A well know motivational speaker, Will Bowen, is quoted as saying, "Complaining is like bad breath. You notice it when it comes out of somebody else's mouth, but not your own."

My breath must have knocked him over. I was speaking about a brother priest to another priest. "I can't stand the way he runs things." I was saying, "If I was in charge, I would ...." And then I told him how if I was in charge, every meeting would be run efficient, productive, and short. In fact, I could do such a good job that no one would ever complain about coming to one of my meetings! Perhaps even world peace, or at least peace in the diocese, would be secure if I was in charge!

"I really think he is doing a good job. I know I couldn't do better," my brother priest told me, silencing my complaining tongue. Embarrassed, I tried to wiggle out of the conversation by shifting the subject to a future event.

Returning to my office, I began to think about my grievances against the priest. Why was I complaining?

Realizing complaining is the end result of comparing and competing, I put my thumb on what was happening in my heart. I felt intimidated by his abilities and position. I was comparing my talents and position, and was coming up short in my mind, which disturbed me. When unsettled, I either retreat or compete. Naturally when I compete, then I complain.

One activity I enjoy is hiking in the mountains. In climbing or hiking on clear days, while the trail might be difficult, as long as the goal is in sight, the mood of the climbers is buoyant. This mood often changes in

dreary, foggy days, where the goal of the summit is always hidden. On these foggy days, not only is our goal veiled, but our understanding of our location in relation to the goal is unseen.

If only we can see as God sees. "But the LORD said to Samuel, "Do not look at his appearance or at the height of his stature, because I have rejected him; for God sees not as man sees, for man looks at the outward appearance, but the LORD looks at the heart."(1 Samuel 16:7) If we could see ourselves as God sees us and realize the joys of heaven, our goal then, what talents we have or don't have, what positions we have or don't have, will make absolutely no difference.

Saint Ignatius of Loyola is credited to suggesting the following way to pray: Look at God, look at you.

"Before I formed you in the womb, I knew you..."
(Jeremiah 1:5)

To see things and ourselves as God sees takes practice and prayer. Even the holy ones of the past struggled with this. I think of two stories in the scriptures.

> "When the servant of the man of God rose early in the morning and went out, behold, an army with horses and chariots was all around the city. And the servant said, 'Alas, my master! What shall we do?' He said, 'Do not be afraid, for those who are with us are more than those who are with them.' Then Elisha prayed and said, 'O Lord, please open his eyes that he may see.' So the Lord opened the eyes of the young man, and he saw, and behold, the mountain was full of horses and chariots of fire all around Elisha." (2 Kings 6:15-17)

Same reality, two different visions of it.

> "Meanwhile the disciples were urging him, saying, 'Rabbi, eat.' But he said to them, 'I have food to eat that you do not know about.' (John 4:31) The Disciples, like us, couldn't see clearly.

Comparing, competing, and complaining.

If only we could see how blessed we are. See through the eyes of our Lord. Then we would be filled with gratitude, and "a grateful heart silences a complaining tongue."

32 YOU CAN LEARN A LOT FROM THE MONASTERY

Let all guests who arrive be received like Christ, for He is going to say, "I came as a guest, and you received Me" (Matt. 25:35). And to all let due honor be shown, especially to the domestics of the faith and to pilgrims. Rule of St. Benedict #53

Where do parents go to get away from the children? Dads go to the garage and mothers go to the bathroom. Where do parish priests go to get away from their parishioners....not Hawaii, that's for sure!

On a Hawaiian cruse for my parent's 50th anniversary, my brother and I took an excursion to a volcano. Hawaii is about 3,600 miles from the parish so I thought I would be safe from inquiring

THE VIEW FROM THE RECTORY WINDOW

parishioners. I was not even dressed as a "priest on vacation." This style is when a priest wears a collar dress shirt but with black pants, black shoes, black belt, and normally black socks (although as priests get older, sometimes they are blue socks and even occasionally white!). Basically the "priest on vacation" style is taking off the clerical shirt and putting on a dress shirt and we think no one will recognize us in such camouflage.

No, I was in shorts and a polo shirt. Very unusual for me, but when in Rome, dress as the Romans. Since I was in Hawaii, and they were sold out of men's lava sarong wraps, and I did not have the necessary chiseled abs to wear one, I was incognito wearing shorts and a polo shirt.

Leaning over the observation deck among no more than eight other tourists, I was shocked to hear the familiar chapel voice. A "chapel voice" is a hushed, drawled out voice of a parishioner trying to get your attention while you are praying in church without wanting to disturb you. "Faaather Keeennn???" I heard in a whispery voice. Thinking perhaps my brother was pulling my leg, I ignored it.

Then I heard it again. "Faaather Kennn???" I knew I was not mistaken. Sure enough, as I turned around from the railing, I recognized a parishioner who also traveled the 3,600 miles from Kansas to this remote volcano, only to find his pastor. Good thing he was on his best behavior. The observation deck was too small, just like the world, and I would have eventually seen him even if he didn't call my name.

VOLUME II

So where do priests go to get away? The monastery of course! In a chapel dedicated to Saint John Vianney there are a series of glass windows depicting his life. The beautiful windows portrayed him preaching, visiting the sick, and other holy endeavors, but I felt like it was missing the most important event in his life. His running away to the monastery!

John Vianney was a parish priest in Ars France in the 19th century. He was known for his extreme holiness and his wisdom in the confessional. He also struggled at times with life in the parish. The parishioners were not always grateful for his austere life or his preaching against many of their favorite vices. In response the Curate (Father) Vianney tried three times to run away from the parish in Ars to the monastery, though returning each time to his post at the parish.

One of the tactics of the devil is to entice a person to keep looking over the fence of his neighbor. It's always greener on the other side. For a parish priest, the other side of the fence is monastic life. In the monastery, a parish priest sees men living in community, security, with time for prayer, and a peaceful atmosphere. It most certainly is all of those things....at least when you are visiting there.

Of course living in monastic life one realizes the monastery is a community of people whom you can't choose (some you like, some you don't), its secure because you can't leave, you are so busy with both community work and outside ministries you feel like there is no time for prayer, and the peaceful atmosphere is not always found in the inside of one's heart.

So where does the monk go to get away? To the parish or secular world, I suspect! This all being said, one can learn a great deal of how to embrace life from the monastery. What follows are some observations I've made while retreating from parish life in monasteries, and how we might apply the monastic life to the lives the Lord has asked us to live.

MISTAKES........

We all make mistakes, but do we publically acknowledge them? What would happen if after you cut someone off in traffic, you tracked them down and apologized? Of course this would never happen, but if you cut someone off at the grocery store with a shopping cart you wouldn't hesitate to excuse yourself.

What's the difference? It's all about a relationship. Driving two tons of plastic and fiberglass (we used to say two tons of metal) we feel very anonymous and superior. We don't have to apologize or excuse ourselves. Cutting someone off in a store with a fifteen pound metal cart, we see each other eye to eye. It's a different relationship. We apologize, even if it's not our fault!

Brother Bernard at Morning Prayer obviously did not have his coffee before we gathered in choir. Not even sure if monks have coffee before Morning Prayer, but Brother Bernard could have used some. He was the cantor, who leads the other monks in the chant. He was not off key, as were many of us, no he was on the wrong page. Wrong week as a matter of fact! Threw everyone off scrambling to find where he was.

Realizing his error, he corrected it, but then after the Morning Prayer was over, he did a peculiar thing. As the other monks filed out of the choir stalls, he knelt down on his knees before the altar and before his brother monks as each one of them filled past him. He was humbling himself before his community for his mistake.

Weather the mistake was in not being prepared, or perhaps another monk had inadvertently set the book incorrectly, nonetheless, Brother Bernard took the responsibility of the error and offered a very quiet, yet profound apology to his community. Wow!

If we did this driving to work, none of us would ever get there, we would all be on our knees in bowed humility. Not good for traffic patterns.

"Humble yourselves before the Lord, and he will lift you up." James 4:10

DISTINCT FROM THE WORLD, YET....

"Wholly ordered to contemplation of the sacred mysteries" is how one website describes the daily life of a Cistercian monk or nun. This is not a new thought to the Cistercians who began over 900 years ago. Aristotle said the "contemplative life is most proper to man; it is also the best and most pleasant..."

We are all called to live a contemplative life, meaning directing our whole attention and gaze to God in whatever we do, whether this is in a monastery or in the secular world. One manner in which we live a contemplative life is to work in the world, while not looking like we are working for the world, but rather for the world yet to come.

We had just completed Mass. Some of the monks continued to pray in the chapel, while others filed out of the abbey church. I being a visitor did my obligatory time in the church after Mass. This means, I prayed my prayers of thanksgiving after Mass not taking too long so I don't look too holy; nor too short, making myself look unholy. Ahh, such pressure!

After my prayers of thanksgiving, I wondered where the monks went. Lunch would not be served for another 15 minutes, so I wondered what the monks did in between times. Perhaps they went to their cells (bedrooms). Perhaps the library? Or maybe the community room (oratory). Since I was not a member of the community, I thought I would simply hang out in the Cloister Walk (hallway) outside the refractory (dining room). Do you notice they have neat names for everything?

Rounding the corner, I bumped into Brother Sebastian. Excusing myself, I realized he was not alone. Looking beyond Brother Sebastian I counted no less than twenty monks. Silently, eyes cast down, at total peace, they were simply waiting. All waiting for the mid-day meal without looking like they were waiting. I'm not sure how they did it, but they were not fidgety, talkative, or anxious. They simply were waiting as only one who lives a contemplative life can.

I took a spot near the stairs and leaned against the banister. After a few minutes, Brother Sebastian silently stepped over. Leaning closer to my ear with his mouth, he quietly said, "You might move from here. Come over here with me."

Thinking I was in trouble, my mind went to several conclusions. Perhaps I was on a sacred place which only the abbot stood. Maybe I was leaning against a bannister that was not solid. Or worse yet, possibly I was standing where visitors were not allowed, and was being ushered to another part of the monastery to my proper place.

"....and he said to him, 'Friend, how did you come in here without wedding clothes?' And he was speechless...." Matthew 22:12

I followed Brother Sebastian only a few feet down to the other side of the hall, with the stairs and bannister in full view. Quietly we waited. My heart racing thinking I had done something terribly wrong, and I tried to be like the other monks: waiting without looking like I was waiting.

Then I heard it. It started quietly at first, but then increased in volume. It sounded like chains were being pulled. Is the place haunted? Then after the chain noise stopped, the most booming chimes I have ever heard in my life began. It was the huge grandfather clock sounding the chimes for noon. Twelve times it bonged. I am quite sure it was heard into the next county! Had I remained where I was standing before Brother Sebastian moved me, I would have been overwhelmed by the rolling thunder it produced. Rolled over by the waves of sound becoming deaf, I am certain.

The silence was broken, and a before meal prayer was prayed and then we entered into the noon meal. The largest meal of the day. The Mass, the time in the hallway, the surprising sound of the clock, and finally the wonderful mid-day meal, all lead me to see how it was a metaphor of our lives, and how the banquet of the noon day meal was the feast of heaven.

Distinct from the world, yet in the world. Waiting as if not waiting. All hallmarks of a contemplative life. But do beware of where you stand in the contemplative life, for you might become deaf!

"To You, O Lord, I call; My rock, do not be deaf to me, For if You are silent to me, I will become like those who go down to the pit." Psalm 28:1

BE PREPARED!!!

As a boy scout I learned the motto, "Be Prepared." But at the monastery I never felt prepared. A diocesan priest prays the Liturgy of the Hours five times a day like a monk, but generally it is between apostolic work, such as confessions, celebrating the Mass, visiting the sick, or taking a nap. (Oops, did I let that slip out?)

Our brievery, or Liturgy of the Hours book is pretty easy to get around once you have done it a couple of years. But at the monastery, the prayers are the same, but the book is different. Not only is the book different, they use more than one book! At the same time!

Sliding into the choir stalls, which really you can't slide because they are literally stalls. Like horse stalls. Separate seats, portioned from one another. Every mother's dream sitting arrangement for her children on long car trips. Sitting down in my assigned stall early to get all the books in order, I noticed in front of me all the books neatly arranged, with the ribbons sticking out so I could readily follow the prayer.

Looking to my side, I saw Brother Gabriel whose head was deep into his chest. Asleep? Probably not, but definitely in repose. I was grateful knowing he had set up my books so I wasn't distracting everyone flipping pages and turning books aside trying to keep up.

Settling into the stall, I was thinking I was special and perhaps Brother Gabriel liked me and therefore helped me out but then I noticed across the sanctuary another monk setting up the liturgical books for his neighbor. Thinking it would be another bewildered guest, I was surprised to see a long time member of the community coming to sit there.

What did the elderly monk then do? Instead of sitting there content that his books were set up like I did, he in turn set up the books for his neighbor, who was also another monk. This went on from one stall to another until the organ began, signifying the beginning of Morning Prayer.

Helping some hapless diocesan priest guest is one thing, but helping someone who doesn't need the help is another. What an example I learned. One of helping out a neighbor, just as we were helped.

"Do to others as you would have them do to you." Luke 6:31

Yes, you can learn a lot from the monastery. Mistakes, contemplative life, helping one another. I also learned there is nothing lost as a lesson from the Lord. One particular elderly monk, Brother Thomas, had the habit of exasperating his brothers by either being places they did not expect, such as giving guests tours in private areas of the monastery interrupting monks at work, or when they wanted him, he is absent.

The abbot, looking for Brother Thomas, and failing to find him said, "Brother Thomas is like the Risen Christ. He appears here, and then is gone again, only to appear again later."

You can learn a lot at the monastery.

"Listen carefully, my child, to your master's precepts, and incline the ear of your heart (Prov. 4:20). Receive willingly and carry out effectively your loving father's advice, that by the labor of obedience you may return to Him from whom you had departed by the sloth of disobedience." Prologue of the Rule of Saint Benedict

33 PRIESTS AND THEIR MOTHERS

On the third day there was a wedding in Cana in Galilee, and the mother of Jesus was there. Jesus and his disciples were also invited to the wedding. When the wine ran short, the mother of Jesus said to him, "They have no wine." John 2: 1-3

The relationship between a mother and a son is always distinctive. But the relationship between a priest and his mother often accents this special relationship.

"So, I understand you have a new priest at your parish?" a woman casually said to another in the gym locker room where they were preparing for their aerobics class. *"What's he like?"* The other women responds, telling her all about the new priest and pastor not knowing she was offering her thoughts of the new pastor to the new pastor's mother!

Not all mothers of priests are so ornery, but none the less they are protective of their sons.

Perhaps this is because of the old and venerable tradition where a newly ordained priest presents his mother with his manitergium. The manutergium, from the Latin manu = tergium = hand towel, is a long cloth used in the Pre-Vatican II rite of ordination. It was wrapped around the hands of the newly ordained priest after the bishop had anointed his hands with the sacred Chrism. The purpose was to prevent excess oil from dripping onto vestments or the floor.

According to this tradition, the mother of a priest is to keep this cloth in a safe place. When she is buried, the cloth is placed in her hands. Then, according to pious legend, when the mother of a priest finally meets our Lord face to face and is asked *"Did you love me?"*, she can reply in the favorably, presenting as part of our cause, her Chrism fragranced hands from the manitergium. Thus showing she loved our Lord so much, she gave Him one of her sons to serve Him as a priest.

Saint Pope Pius X wrote, *"A vocation comes from the heart of God, but goes through the heart of the mother."* This is true of all vocations, but especially that of a priest. As a priest, we must be a parent, that is, a mother and a father. There are times when gentleness is called for in the confessional or the tender wisdom of a mother in the hospital room with an elderly parishioner.

Sometimes the manly strength of a father figure is needed in the pulpit or the "man who is still a boy" father is needed to play on the playground slide with the children is needed. A parish priest often is the only father the children have on a daily basis! To be a parish priest is to be a parent: mother and father.

But a mother of a priest shares in the priesthood of her son in a like manner in which Mary stood at the foot of the cross. She cannot be the Simon of Cyrene, carrying her son's cross. She cannot be John the Apostle who walked with Jesus in preaching. No, a mother of a priest is at the beginning of a priest's ministry before ordination, encouraging like Mary did at Cana. (John 2) She also silently walks with her son and is a presence at his passion. (John 19:25) Whether that passion is being misunderstood by parishioners even though she warned him "Not everyone is going to get your humor son!" or when he is grieving having been moved from one parish community to another.

She will stand often in place of Mary whom Jesus gave to His church and in particular His priests: *"Woman, behold your son."* (John 19:26) Sometimes the mother of a priest is like Mary at the Feast of Cana, *"Son, they have no wine."* (John 2:3) Frequently parishioners will intersect with a mother of a priest, telling her all of their troubles of why they don't attend Church or Mass any longer. The mother of a priest intuitively knows the archetypal response, *"Go to my son. He is a priest. He will help you."* I don't know how many calls or visits I've had in my quarter century of priesthood which began, *"I was talking to a woman in the waiting room (gym, store, etc.) and she told me she was your mother and that I should talk with you and you would help me...."*

This uniqueness of this relationship between a priest and his mother was recently accentuated to me. Looking through a library of a priest who had passed away, I noticed a very old, turn of the century edition of Saint Francis de Sales book, *"Introduction to the Devout Life."* Inside the front cover was a penned inscription. Obviously the book was a gift from the priest son to his mother. Here is what it said:

To Mother.

This little book, O Mother Dear,
Contains much counsel, wise and clear,
Which, by God's grace, this holy saint
Has giv'n to free us from all taint.

If then, this helps you in your trails
To dodge the devil's snares and wiles
And guides you heav'nward on life's way
'Tis the best I can give you on Mother's Day.

Your loving son, Quintin

This is what the special relationship is all about: the faith generously given to the son is then returned to the mother. "Woman, behold your son. Son, behold your mother."

Today the manitergium cloth is not used in the rite of ordination, so many of the newly ordained priests will carry a small embroidered cloth and wipe the excess oil onto it, giving it to their mothers. (I must have missed this directive in the seminary...ah the 80's!. Sorry Mom! I wonder if a hand written note would work? But I suspect, He already knows....)

But the greatest gift any priest or child can give their mother is the gift of faith. This gift from a mother now given to children, parishioners, and even returned to a parent. That which was given and received, is then lived and gratefully shared with others.

This is all a mother would want!

34 MY SON, MY BROTHER, MY FATHER

"As well as in the wilderness, where you saw how the LORD, your God, carried you, as one carries his own son, all along your journey until you arrived at this place." (Deut. 1:31)

It was a transition he traversed easily. First I was his son, now his father. It was a transition he made over twenty years before, but we were living out in a real way at the end. "He" was my father; I was his son...his parish priest and pastor.

It is unusual for a priest to be assigned to his home parish or to the parish of his family. Biblical precedents are not too keen or successful for these placements. Such as, *"He departed from there and came to his native place, accompanied by his disciples. When the Sabbath came he began to teach in the synagogue, and many who heard him were astonished. They said, "Where did this man get all this? What kind of wisdom has been given him? What mighty deeds are wrought by his hands! Is he not the carpenter, the son of Mary, and the brother of James and Joses and Judas and Simon? And are not his sisters here with us?" And they took offense at him."* (Mark 6:1-4)

There are other examples such as Joseph of the Old Testament being rejected by his brothers (Gen 37:5-11) and then not even recognized by his brothers when he saved them (Gen 42); or the shepherd David not being recognized by his father as being in the pool of candidates to be chosen as king (1 Samuel 16:1-12). Even Saint Joseph was hesitant to recognize the actions of the Lord in his new family, his betrothed, *"Joseph her husband, since he was a righteous man, yet unwilling to expose her to shame, decided to divorce her quietly."* (Matthew 1:19)

'Familiarity breeds contempt' the old proverb states. But there are times when a priest or prophet does get sent to his home town, among the familiar. A person such as Father Emil Kapaun was assigned to his home parish of Pilsen, Kansas in 1940. His cause for sainthood is being promoted now. Or Padre Pio who for a long time after ordination due to illness remained at home. But these are exceptions.

For my father, the transition seemed effortless. I remember him introducing me to others as: "This is my son, who is my brother (Knights of Columbus) and my father (pastor)." And He did so with a smile of pleasure. I felt good about it all.

He worked first as a florist then for the international company, IBM. I remember well the time I went to see where he worked and what he did. Proudly he would introduce me as his son. I do not think I was old enough to understand what he did, but do remember all the neat forms and papers he would bring home for me to play with. I would pretend to be him at work, playing at a desk in the basement in our 1920's bungalow home. Interestingly, this was the same basement I converted into a chapel, using crackers as bread, and tracing my own homemade stations of the cross on sheets of IBM white paper to be placed around the "chapel" walls, so I could pretend to say Mass.

Fathers have a great influence on their children. I realize this more and more now, especially as I write this reflection behind a desk in an office on a computer. All the while that computer sits on a desk in an office that is located in a Church! Funny how our Lord works!

*Certainly sons are a gift from the LORD, the fruit of
the womb, a reward.*
*Like arrows in the hand of a warrior are the sons
born in one's youth.*
*Blessed is the man who has filled his quiver with
them.*
*He will never be shamed for he will destroy his foes
at the gate.* (Psalm 127: 3-5)

The passing on of the Faith is greatly influenced by
a father. A great example of this is in the life of Karol
Woytyla (Pope Saint John Paul II). He lost his mother
when he was nine years old and subsequently he
spent much of this time with his father, even sharing a
bedroom at night.

Young Karol recalls waking up in the early hours,
way before dawn, and seeing his father kneeling,
deeply absorbed in prayer. This example of his father
left an indelible impression on the future pope and
saint. His earthly father had a deep and intimate
relationship with God the Father and passed this onto
his son.

I too remember the figure of my father over the
kitchen sink: toast in one hand, his devotional in the
other. Or the many times I, as a child, would fall
asleep on his lap during Mass or Stations of the Cross.
But the most vivid memory was praying the rosary
with him in his last months, only to have him
apologize for not having the strength to vocalize his
words. I assured him, he who gave me a voice in this
world, was giving voice for him in the next.

At the end of his life, I had the honor of giving him Viaticum, which is the Last Rites of the Church. This "Bread for the journey," Holy Communion, was consecrated by me and brought to his house. What a privilege it was to serve him in this way.

I always wondered how my father so seamlessly accepted me, his son, as his father. In going through his prayer book I found tucked in the front a prayer card I had never seen before which perhaps held a clue. On the front was a drawing of a priest lifting up the Eucharist saying "Hoc est corpus meum!" (This is my Body!) But on the backside was this prayer:

Oh, it seems to me, this morning,
That my troubles all have ceased,
For I have some news to tell you;
I'm the father of a priest.

Once, I thought my heart was bursting
With the crowding of its joy,
When the first time, pink and helpless,
In the arms I held my boy.
But that joy was but a trifle-
What a crumb is to a feast-
To the gladness of this morning:
I'm the father of a priest.

Yes, his hands lay on me, blessing,
And his voice was low and glad,
When I whispered, "Your Rev'rence"
And he answered, "My Dear Dad."
And I know God will be gentle
When my poor soul is released,
For I'll tell Him, "Blessed Savior,
I have given you a Priest."
(St. Joseph's Press)

In our search for God, our fathers play a key role. I know mine did in my life. It is my hope and faith, that when I enter into my last stages of life and move to see the face of God, my father will be there to introduce me to the Lord and say:

"He whom You gave to me long ago, I now return to You, for this son of yours is also my son, my brother, and my father. Welcome him as you have welcomed me."

"In my Father's house are many rooms. If it were not so, would I have told you that I go to prepare a place for you?" (John 14:2)

CONCLUSION

"Go, therefore, and make disciples of all nations, baptizing them in the name of the Father, and of the Son, and of the holy Spirit." Matthew 28:19

Every one of us has stories. Stories of how the Lord interacts in our lives. How another has lead us to the Lord. Growing up, my mother would strategically leave different Catholic or Christian magazines in the bathroom. These magazines were mainly comprised of stories of conversion and of faith. I believe they were instrumental in my vocation to the priesthood and life of faith today.

Without stories of conversion and faith, we would question if God really worked in our world today. Perhaps God stopped intervening in the world once He got finished with Moses, Abraham, and Jesus. Perhaps the death of the last Apostle, John, God took a long nap. Not true!

While the Bible will not record our experiences of God, they are no less important to our lives of faith, and to the lives of our families and friends. It is my hope through my writing of my experiences of seeing the Lord's works through my vocation of the priesthood; others will begin to see how the Lord works through their lives, and then most importantly share it with family and friends.

We share these experiences not to say, "Hey, look at me! I've got my act together." No, rather we share our experiences of the Lord with one another so that "we may be mutually encouraged by each other's faith..." (Romans 1:12) and so we may be acknowledged by Him.

"I tell you, whoever publicly acknowledges me before others, the Son of Man will also acknowledge before the angels of God..." (Luke 12:8-9)

Now, go proclaim your own story!

ABOUT THE AUTHOR

Father Ken VanHaverbeke was ordained for the Catholic Diocese of Wichita [Kansas] in 1991 and has served as a parish priest/pastor and various diocesan ministries including retreat work, deaf ministry, and ministering to priests.

Made in the USA
Charleston, SC
05 April 2016